REVELS STUDENT EDITIONS

THE WHITE DEVIL
John Webster

MANCHESTER
1824

Manchester University Press

REVELS STUDENT EDITIONS

Based on the highly respected Revels Plays, which provide a wide range of scholarly critical editions of plays by Shakespeare's contemporaries, the Revels Student Editions offer readable and competitively priced introductions, text and commentary designed to distil the erudition and insights of the Revels Plays, while focusing on matters of clarity and interpretation. These editions are aimed at undergraduates, graduate teachers of Renaissance drama and all those who enjoy the vitality and humour of one of the world's greatest periods of drama.

GENERAL EDITOR David Bevington

REVELS STUDENT EDITIONS

THE WHITE DEVIL
John Webster

Edited by John Russell Brown

based on The Revels Plays edition
edited by John Russell Brown
published by Methuen & Co., 1960
and by Manchester University Press, 1977

MANCHESTER
UNIVERSITY PRESS
Manchester and New York

distributed in the United States exclusively by
Palgrave Macmillan

Introduction, critical apparatus, etc.
© John Russell Brown 1996

The right of John Russell Brown to be identified as the editor of this work
has been asserted by him in accordance with the Copyright, Designs and
Patents Act 1988.

Published by Manchester University Press
Oxford Road, Manchester M13 9NR, UK
and Room 400, 175 Fifth Avenue, New York, NY 10010, USA
www.manchesteruniversitypress.co.uk

Distributed in the United States exclusively by
Palgrave Macmillan, 175 Fifth Avenue, New York,
NY 10010, USA

Distributed in Canada exclusively by
UBC Press, University of British Columbia, 2029 West Mall,
Vancouver, BC, Canada V6T 1Z2

British Library Cataloguing-in-Publication Data
A catalogue record for this book is available from the British Library

Library of Congress Cataloging-in-Publication Data applied for

ISBN 978 0 7190 4355 0 *paperback*

First published 1996

16 15 14 13 12 11 10   12 11 10 9 8 7 6

The publisher has no responsibility for the persistence or accuracy of
URLs for external or any third-party internet websites referred to in this
book, and does not guarantee that any content on such websites is, or
will remain, accurate or appropriate.

Typeset
by Best-set Typesetter Ltd, Hong Kong

Printed in Great Britain
by Bell & Bain Ltd, Glasgow

Introduction

At its first performance early in 1612, *The White Devil* was not well received. Later the same year, when the text was published, the author declared that the Queen's Men had never acted better and that his friend, Richard Perkins, had had a triumph; it would be more than ten years before this actor, now in his early thirties, had a comparable success, but here 'the worth of his action did crown both the beginning and end'. Yet something had gone wrong: in a preface to 'To the Reader', Webster trashed both his audience as 'ignorant asses' and the theatre, the Red Bull, as too 'open and black' for this play, especially in winter time. Presumably he would have preferred one of the indoor 'private' theatres, with more select audiences. The script was rushed into print, so that readers could judge for themselves. The author provided his own manuscript, and visited the press to make corrections and add further explanatory stage directions.

At this time, Webster was about thirty-two years of age and had been writing for at least ten years. But so far he had published only a few occasional verses, and his work for the stage had been limited to collaboration with other writers, helping to supply plays which had to be written within a few weeks of being commissioned. *The White Devil* was his first full-length and unaided bid for success. 'To those who report I was a long time in finishing this tragedy', he wrote to the reader, 'I confess I do not write with a goose-quill'— nothing foolish or brainlessly imitative in *his* drama. The whole preface has an air of injured pride and disappointed hope. Thomas Dekker, one of his earlier and more experienced co-authors, had written a short preview for this exceptional play in a preface to one of his own, wishing well for its 'brave triumphs of poesy and elaborate industry'; such a play deserved 'a theatre full of very Muses themselves to be spectators'.

In some ways the Red Bull in Clerkenwell must have seemed the appropriate venue for *The White Devil*. It was Webster's local theatre, about half a mile to the north of where he lived inside the

1

city wall at Smithfield; and he seems to have kept its audience in mind as he wrote. Local and topical references abound in the script, such as that to the amateurish city militia in training at the Artillery Yard, a practice revived in 1610 and not made official until July 1612, a few months after *The White Devil* had been first performed; this was introduced, to give a flash of immediate recognition, in the very last scene (l. 160); so too were lions in the zoo at the Tower of London, together with a reference to the bad weather (ll. 265–8). When Bracciano dies earlier in the same act, there are allusions to the pest-house erected for those sick of the plague in 1594 and to expectations of a 'new river' bringing fresh water to the city which had begun building in 1609 and would not be finished until Michaelmas 1613 (V.iii.178, 184). And here, as this Italian nobleman is being murdered in his palace at Padua, are more general references to the city life of London: to dog-killers who coped with mad dogs, to tight-rope walkers who entertained the crowds, to rat-catchers, market produce, good bargains, and scores run-up in taverns, to threshers, nurses, men in liveries, and drunken priests (see annotations, V.iii.95–212). Such topical and local references have always been hallmarks of popular theatre and are not usually associated with 'brave triumphs' of a superior 'poesy'.

Webster must have known and tried to please the audience for which he was writing. The Red Bull had a reputation for providing clowns, fights (on stage and off) and spectacle; and Webster, for all his artistic ambition, seems to have gone out of his way to provide a full quota of these. *The White Devil* has its comic cuckold, crazy doctor and grotesquely loquacious lawyer. It has a ghost, an apparition, two dumb shows, several processions, celebratory fights at the 'barriers', weird disguises, rituals, murders, cold-blooded torture. There are two mad-scenes and another pretended one, a sensational trial and the election of a corrupt cardinal as Pope with all appropriate formalities.

The dramatist might have been known personally by some of the tradesmen and apprentices who made up the majority of the audience at this theatre. His father, John Webster senior, was an established coachmaker and member of the Merchant Taylors Company of the City of London, and he took an active role in local affairs. His thriving trade was highly visible as it supplied a growing demand for transport in the over-crowded and rapidly expanding capital. The Webster firm hired out coaches, as well as making them (Alleyn, the actor, was one of its customers); it also supplied wagons for Lord

Mayor shows, hearses for funerals and carts to take criminals on their way to public hanging at Tyburn. While a younger son, Edward, was apprenticed to the trade and eventually took over the family business, the elder son's meagre literary output makes it all but certain that he too was actively employed in it, in order to provide himself with a reasonable income. The playwright, John junior, had probably attended the Merchant Taylors' School (run by his father's guild and one of the best schools in London) and may well have been the John Webster who was admitted to study law at the Middle Temple in 1598; he would then have been in training for the administrative and litigious side of the business, one vital to its success. This would explain why Henry Fitzjeffrey's satirical verses, published in 1618, call a 'crabbed Websterio' the 'Playwright, Cartwright' (*Certain Elegies done by Sundry Excellent Wits*). In 1605, at the age of twenty-six, he had married Sara Peniall, daughter of a neighbouring saddler and a warden of their company (a trade associated with coachmaking); she was only seventeen and already seven months pregnant. Within a few years, several children had increased the need for a regular income.

Obviously John Webster knew the city well and wrote his first play with a city audience in mind. But his imagination was mostly else-where, in writing, constant reading (and making copious notes as he did so), and observing closely and sceptically the affairs of the Court of King James I. *The White Devil* is pre-eminently about 'Great Men' and the operation of privilege and authority. Its main characters are concerned with success, money, and power, whether these are gained by driving ambition, spilling of blood or exploitation of sexual attractiveness and desire, or gained by the plain good fortune of being born to rich parents who did not waste their wealth before they died. It provides a parade of busy, knowledgeable, and conniving adventurers, seeking their own satisfaction, taunted by insecurity and threatened by almost everyone they encounter. When they are not pursuing actively their own advantage at the court, the place of authority, judgement and privilege, they surreptitiously watch others: 'This busy trade of life appears most vain, / Since rest breeds rest, where all seek pain by pain' (V.vi.273–4). So Flamineo sums up his life and the world in which he lives; and it is possible that by that 'rest' which is bred by rest, he may mean not peace and quiet but finality and death.

Webster's first tragedy is set in Italy nearly thirty years earlier, and it tells the story of Bracciano, a noble duke, and of his mistress,

Vittoria, who had come to Rome as bride of Camillo, nephew of a cardinal who had 'bought' her from her father. The duke's passion is so strong that he arranges the murder of Camillo and of Isabella, his own wife; Vittoria seems to be the first to suggest this line of action. After she has been arraigned and imprisoned as a whore, Bracciano escapes with her to Padua where they are married. Then both are murdered separately, at the instigation of powerful relatives of their earlier victims. Flamineo, Vittoria's brother, is also killed; as Bracciano's secretary, he had advanced his sister's fortunes as a means of making his own. The essentials of this story were known all over Europe—well over a hundred early manuscripts have come to light in various libraries and private collections—but Webster was not content to follow any one source. He used at least three versions, and went further afield for some particular incidents. His research would be impressive even by scholarly standards of today, but to serve his purposes this exotic, sensational and sometimes mysterious story had to be retold very carefully. It was Webster's means, not for showing a recent event in a foreign country so that it would be accurate in every detail, but for depicting the political and moral state of England in his own day. The Italian setting, with its detailed allusions to Italian families, men of religion and political leaders, ceremonies and day-to-day habits and procedures, was a pretence that allowed Webster to evade the strict censorship that had landed Ben Jonson and other dramatists in prison for showing too clearly their criticism of King James I and of his family, favourites, ministers and courtiers—the apparatus of authority in England.

Of course there is no portrait of King James in Webster's play. Even well disguised, that would have been impossible; it would have prevented any performance of his script and possibly finished his career. Rather than that, Webster put Vittoria at the centre of his play: a white devil; a challenging image of power, intelligence, and mysterious attractiveness; a dazzling clash of good and evil; in biblical language, Satan transformed into an Angel of Light; in theatrical terms, a sensational innovation. Vittoria enters the stage in only six scenes, but each time she is in a different guise: first as mistress to Bracciano, who admits himself 'quite lost' for love of her; then as the accused at the bar of an ecclesiastical court; then as prisoner in a 'house of penitent whores'; and then, transformed spectacularly, as a bride who maintains a total silence. Her next appearance is at Bracciano's deathbed and then, finally, she is discovered at her prayers and is murdered, exposing her breast to the assassin's sword. Through all these episodes, Vittoria is amazing, in her physical, sensual, emotional and intellectual resources. No earlier play in English had been so dominated by a woman who set herself against the expectations of society, religion and the law—not even *Antony and Cleopatra*, because its adulterous heroine dies in royal style by her own hand, calling on her lover as 'husband'.

Vittoria is given many names in the course of the play, by others and by herself: 'counterfeit jewel', 'mine of diamonds', 'notorious strumpet', 'fury', 'whirlwind', 'my dearest happiness', 'this good woman', 'a blazing ominous star', 'glorious strumpet', 'a most prodigious comet'. But she has no long death-speech in which to sum up her nature or intentions; instead several are given to Flamineo who is given time to acknowledge a greater spirit than his own:

> Th' art a noble sister—
> I love thee now; if woman do breed man
> She ought to teach him manhood.   (V.vi.241-3)

At her death, as she keeps pace with her restless and unappeased mind, Vittoria has a sequence of short speeches, but they are contradictory and seemingly unconnected. Her last words are not about herself; they bring the audience's thoughts back to the court—the court of King James, at least as much as the courts of Italy: 'O happy they that never saw the court, / Nor ever knew great man but by report' (V.vi.261-2). In no way can such a couplet sum up the subtle presentation of this tragic heroine; it runs too smoothly and conventionally. But it did issue a challenge to members of the audience to consider the seat of administrative power in the land and its effect upon their own lives.

Webster did dare to bring on stage the English Ambassador to observe the carnage of the play's last moments and to call out 'Keep back the prince.—Shoot, shoot!'. Perhaps this also helped to bring the experience back to immediate concerns since, at this time, the young Prince Henry, eldest son of James I, offered new hope to those who had little or none in his father's court and government. The prince was to die in November 1612, his promise unfulfilled; and the next year Webster published an elegy in praise of him, returning to the same theme in *Monuments of Honour* eleven years later, when there could no longer be hope of reward for praising a teenage prince.

Flamineo is the character who brings the play closest to the real political situation at the court of King James. He is the highly intelligent and apparently amoral secretary to the great Duke

Bracciano, constantly on the look-out for personal advantage, but also desperately cynical about the whole competitive and dangerous business of court life. Webster has placed Flamineo in contact with the audience and kept him there by means of soliloquies and asides which explain his thought-processes, or seem to do so. At the end of the first act, he says that to reach the 'top' he must imitate the 'subtle foldings of a winter's snake . . . winding and indirect' (I.ii.351–5). Halfway through the play, at the end of Act IV, scene ii, he excuses his manipulations and 'varying of shapes' with the uncompromising claim: 'Knaves do grow great by being great men's apes' (IV.ii.245–9). In talk with Francisco, he boasts of the villany he could do safely in 'a fair room yet hung with arras, and some great cardinal to lug me by th'ears as his endeared minion' (V.i.122–6). Flamineo encourages dangerous talk from Francisco, who is here thoroughly disguised as Mulinassar the Moor and so outside the duke's jurisdiction:

> what difference is between the duke and I? No more than between two bricks; all made of one clay. Only't may be one is placed on the top of a turret, the other in the bottom of a well by mere chance. If I were placed as high as the duke, I should stick as fast, make as fair a show, and bear out weather equally.
> (V.i.106–11)

Such ideas would, a few decades later, turn the world upside down and help to precipitate civil war in England. Flamineo gives back some politic instruction: 'The duke says he will give you pension; that's but bare promise; get it under his hand'. In his view the 'miserable courtesy' received at court is like the 'hot cordial drinks' given to prisoners on the rack, who are revived only so that they may endure more torture (V.i.133–42).

The White Devil is a long play, and it needed to be if Webster was to pin down the implications of his exotic and sensational story and engage his audience in the injustice of that court world, close to home, which it reflects. Webster has been blamed for writing too copiously and curiously, but imaginative power and sharp observation are evident even in the most complicated and digressive speeches. If he had a fault in this regard, it is rather that he seldom gave up applying pressure or exploring motives. He wrote like a man determined to establish his own view of the world by any means at his disposal. Yet he also knew the force of simplicity. At crisis-point, when Flamineo reconsiders his actions and motives in a soliloquy packed with observation of court life and fired by his own unprecedented sensations, some thoughts could hardly be more nakedly expressed or more free from tension (see V.iv.114–52). To understand the drive behind the writing of this play, its long disquisitions and illustrations, together with short, instinctive exclamations, must all be studied in detail of text, context and subtext.

Webster knew someone at the court in Whitehall who had a position not unlike Flamineo's. Thomas Overbury, son of a west country lawyer, had been a brilliant student at Queen's College Oxford, and it is likely that he and Webster met when both were student members of the Middle Temple in London, the training ground for courtiers, diplomats and men of letters, as well as for lawyers. Although enrolled the previous year, Overbury would have taken up residence in London after gaining his Oxford B.A. in 1598, the same year as a John Webster was enrolled. If they did not meet then, plenty of opportunities would have come later; Overbury had a wide acquaintance among literary people, including the dramatists Ben Jonson and John Ford, and after Overbury's early death Webster was one of those who contributed to a collection of 'Characters' published under his name in 1615. In 1608, four years before The White Devil's first performance, Overbury had been knighted for serving as friend and adviser to the king's favourite, Robert Carr. This position was much like Flamineo's to Duke Bracciano in Webster's play: Overbury arranged for Carr to meet the Countess of Essex who after a spectacular divorce was to be Carr's wife; he gave constant advice to a master who was generally recognized to be not so clever as himself. Overbury's influence was such that Queen Anne called him Carr's 'Governor'; people who wanted favours from Carr, and so from the king, would first apply to Overbury. By exploiting the king's friendship, Carr became Viscount Rochester in 1611 (the first Scotsman to sit in the House of Lords) and in 1613 he was created Earl of Somerset (the first commoner ennobled in this way since 1579). But by 1616, it was all over; Carr had been condemned to death, his life spared only by the king's intervention. Overbury's story was even shorter: because of scandals and jealousies associated with Carr's amours, he was imprisoned in the Tower of London on 26 April 1613, and there shortly afterwards he died, almost certainly poisoned by the Countess of Essex. That Webster had experienced at first hand the ruthless ambition of these two men can scarcely be doubted; in 1613, he dedicated A Monumental Column, his elegy for Prince Henry, to 'My right Noble Lord', Viscount Rochester, and signed himself 'Your honour's truly devoted servant'; and to know him was to know Overbury. While in his play Webster denounced the 'slippery ice-pavements' of the court, in his professional life he kept carefully in the sun of the king's favourite.

A modern analogy would be the necessary formal and public attention that has been paid to men in power by writers who were, at the same time but more surreptitiously, exposing in their plays the horrors of a ruthless exercise of power in Soviet Russia and other totalitarian regimes in Eastern Europe, South America and else-where. In their daily lives, writers in these modern contexts have had to live with spies (or 'intelligencers', as Webster called them), show trials, misinformation, summary imprisonment, violence, treachery; and they have learned to work in an undercover way, writing plays that are full of suggestion and challenge, and yet of sufficient exag-geration to be passed off to a censor as sheer fantasy or crazy humour.

The choice of Vittoria as hero of the tragedy is in line with such a purpose, for who would dare to say that a 'notorious strumpet' heralded a play that was an attack upon the centre of political power? (Some might privately think that the Countess of Essex, for example, might have earned that name, or that Carr's influence on the king involved much the same morality; but no one was going to bring such charges in public.) Changeable, vital, mysterious, and 'impudent', Vittoria destabilizes the drama in which she appears: her 'brave spirit' and the bitterness of her adversaries (III.ii.140, 107) take confidence and force out of any ready-made moral judgements a member of the audience might have brought to the play. Provo-cative silences ensure that an audience must guess at her private feelings as she triumphs in her marriage or as, earlier, she is recon-ciled to Bracciano in Act IV, scene ii; 'Your dog or hawk should be rewarded better / Than I have been. I'll speak not one word more' (ll. 192–3). Her simplest statements, 'O me accurst!' and 'O me! This place is hell' (I.ii.302 and V.iii.180), and perhaps her last words in that neat couplet already quoted, also demand the audience's active interpretation and judgement.

The courts of Italy were probably unknown to Webster, except in the documents he had studied for his plot and characters, and in books of history, travel, politics and morality. But they inflamed his imagination because they were not dissimilar to what he had seen of the court which was not far from the city where he lived, and which was the centre of government and source of power in his own land, conspicuous in its use of wealth and its need for it. This was a world which Webster knew and understood only too well; he was fascinated and repelled by it, and felt impelled to show others how it functioned and why it was as it was. This gave him a mission and directed the development of his skills. In writing his first tragedy, political concerns were uppermost in his mind and the cause of many of his innovations.

STYLE

Not all scholars and critics agree about this and *The White Devil* is often commended for other reasons—which are equally valid only if the over-reaching political thrust of the writing is ignored or discounted. Passages of 'poetry', swift and inevitable phrases, moments of emotional intensity briefly verbalized, an obsession with death that yields both horror and moral revaluation: these have been offered as achievements to offset the disadvantages of a play that seems wilfully to break all the rules of careful construction, having a 'loose and rambling' structure, a 'gothic aggregation rather than a steady exposition and development towards a single consummation'. Those words are from the Introduction to the original Revels Plays edition of *The White Devil* (1960), which went on to defend the play by claiming that its 'restless technique' was in fact not a fault but its most significant achievement. In this view, the sensibility expressed in its dialogue is the heart of the play, not its form or even its action, still less any identifiable theme or argument beyond the notion that sin is bad and is usually paid for. What is spoken enables the audience to develop, in the course of a performance, an understanding of the author's attitude towards the characters. If Webster's political purpose is discounted, here lies the chief value of the whole play.

In this view, the words of a minor character, Antonelli, serve as a motto for the whole (even though they are placed incidentally, not at the climax of an argument, still less of a scene):

affliction

Expresseth virtue, fully, whether true,
Or else adulterate.   (I.i.49–51)

The Revels Introduction represents this widely held view: 'as we watch, awed and insecure, we will feel pity in our hearts for those who suffer, for those who by pain seek pain; with its horrors, its

deadly laughter and its intricacies, the dramatic experience is humane, and in Vittoria's end ennobling' (p. lviii). These arguments
imply that Webster had chosen to present a fragmentary, decentred
world because he despaired of any heroic action or hopeful resolution. Among recent critics, J. R. Mulryne has written of the 'moral
and emotional anarchy' of the play and Charles Forker has argued
that Webster was working out an 'aesthetics of chaos'.

Other critics searching for a single unifying idea have argued that
Webster was consciously presenting a disordered world without
moral certainty in order to identify endurance or stoical survival
as the greatest of virtues. Travis Bogard used a phrase taken from
Webster's later play, *The Duchess of Malfi*, and explained that *The
White Devil* also extolls an 'integrity of life'. Yet opinions differ as to
what that clear-sounding phrase might have meant in Webster's
day—and even in our own, when we speak more often of 'integrity'.
The rather generalized notion of 'integrity of life' leaves a great
many moral and psychological questions unanswered. More re-
cently, Muriel Bradbrook has written that 'egotism keeps [Webster's
characters] afloat in their uncomprehended several orbits'. The
assumption underlying much of this criticism is that the dramatist
was not primarily interested in particular characters, but rather was
searching for some form of moral gold in unruly moments of horror,
lust, pride and (most notably) ingenuity.

The incidental quality of Webster's writing is not in debate. Even
critics who are most reluctant to praise the sensational and complicated story, or what can be seen as the immoral and unlikely
characters, will praise some of Webster's speeches for amazing sub-
tlety of expression, word play, vivid imagery and haunting rhythms.
The open question is whether these occasional achievements are
the mere flashes and freaks of a literary imagination or the more
noticeable marks of a theatrical imagination which by other means
was able to sustain the long progress of the play. Here the analysis of
verbal imagery and recurrent words associated with the 'New Criticism' of the immediate post-World-War-I years came to Webster's
defence. It soon became obvious that he has played consciously and
fastidiously with certain recurrent ideas indicated by repeated words
and images: 'greatness' and 'great men'; the 'devil in crystal' (the
'white devil' of the play's title); notions of the fair, the holy and the
damned; woman, man, god, and beast (see for example IV.ii.84–
92); soul, body and wit; devils, witches, doctors and saints; 'thinking' as distinct from 'doing', in many variations. These recurrent

and oppositional words are so used and reused, and so intertwined in a subtle net of verbal connections that enmeshes the whole play, that it must have been woven by a distinctive imagination.

Yet when painstaking scholars—notably R. W. Dent—discovered that Webster had lifted whole sections from the works of other writers and that he must have kept a 'commonplace book' in which to note down phrases and sentiments to use on later occasions, it was thought at first that he had merely pieced together these stolen scraps of wisdom—or, some might say, pompous generalities—to give a weighty sententiousness where none was deserved. But on closer inspection, this cannot be the case: each passage Webster introduced is re-tuned for its new context, the moment's mood and, it might be argued, for its speaker. So in Act I, scene ii he used a passage from one of his favourite sources, John Florio's translation of Montaigne's *Essays* (1603): 'they [women] will have fire: . . . Luxury is like a wild beast, first made fiercer with tying, and then let loose.' In *The White Devil*, Flamineo is speaking, and for him Webster has reshaped and enlivened what he had picked up from Florio: 'Come sister, darkness hides your blush. Women are like curst dogs: civility keeps them tied all daytime, but they are let loose at midnight; then they do most good or most mischief' (ll. 199–202). A 'wild beast' has become 'curst dogs'; 'daytime' and 'midnight' have transformed the merely sequential 'first . . . and then'; the generalized 'Luxury' has disappeared and 'fire' yielded to 'most good or most mischief'. This is no lazy borrowing, content with another person's phrases. Some of the 'sentences' taken from other writers are so changed that, were it not known that Webster had borrowed elsewhere from the same place in the same author, the debt might never have been discovered. Clearly Webster brooded on his writing, listening, gathering confidence or dissatisfaction, inventing freely, not easily satisfied. From play to play, Webster also quotes, as it were, from himself, developing, sharpening, or completely altering the force of an image or juxtaposition of words he had previously used elsewhere.

This re-phrasing or re-tuning of what other writers have written points to a defining quality of Webster's verbal style: it has a self-nurturing energy, representing the quickening of thought and utterance as they feed upon each other. Speech in this play mirrors the movement of thought, self-consciousness, and utterance: it is improvisational by its very nature, nervous, continually shifting in confidence and direction. Two techniques are especially important

for achieving this effect. First, ideas and expressions seem sometimes to grow out of each other affectively, as if words are controlled
more by feeling than by logic or rational sequence. There are some
formal speeches, built up with impressive rhetorical structures—a
notable example is Monticelso's 'Character' of a whore (III.ii.78–
101)—but many of the most powerful passages seem to develop
their own energy, taking a course dictated by subtextual currents
of consciousness and by physical engagement. Flamineo's last
speeches exemplify all this: his words react to pain, and to his own
attempts to think of the present and reflect on the past; at times
he seems to be aware of those listening to him on stage and in
the audience, and beyond, and of a need to master his own thoughts
and feelings; aware too of what his sister is saying and of his own
on-coming silence. He seems to speak in order to command or
tame a tortured and alarming consciousness, as if death were occasion for an exercise in self-control. His words are remarkable
in themselves—several times they have an almost proverbial
assurance—but also for the flickering intensity of what drives them,
the impression they give of multiple and changing impulses behind
speech.

Linked to this organic and often unexpected progression in speech
is an idiosyncratic use of punctuation. The first Quarto edition of
the play was set by three compositors from Webster's own auto-
graph manuscript, and he visited the press to oversee the printing,
sometimes interrupting ordinary processes to insist on the alteration
of tiny details in what he had written or was already set in print. The
result is a text with very peculiar punctuation; it may involve a run
of commas where normally one would expect colons, full stops or
marks of exclamation, or a sudden intrusion of colons, or no punctuation at all. Jacobean compositors were remarkably free, by today's standards, to change spelling or punctuation to suit their own
tastes or convenience, but these compositors did not usually set copy
like this. We may be sure that much of the unusual punctuation
derives from their 'copy' which was in the hand of Webster himself.
For this reason any responsible modern edition needs to punctuate
with as much regard for the original as for clarity, and cannot be
content with ordinary modern usages. With the addition of some
dashes and the correction of obvious errors and omissions, a text
punctuated with a prudent measure of respect for the original
edition will come alive as it is spoken with a startling sense of
actuality. An example is that passage where Vittoria is shown the

love-letter that Francisco, the Duke of Florence, has sent her, through to the end of their quarrel (IV.ii.84–207). A text, like this present one, which responds to the Quarto's punctuation, will some-times have short or even abrupt sentences, phrases without verbs treated as independent utterances, sudden breaks after which speech proceeds on a different tack with no hesitation at all, sentences broken in two, apparently arbitrarily but so that an explosive force is given to the new thought. This edition tries to strike a compromise, retaining the original punctuation wherever it will not hinder imme-diate comprehension. No editor can be sure that Webster's original intentions have been preserved in any one instance, but equally certainly following a modern or seventeenth-century rule-book will work against the quick, nervous, intermittent pulse of the writing, its quick responses to action and reaction.

CHARACTERIZATION

Even if so much is granted, it might still be argued that the speakers in this play are creatures of literary and theatrical inventiveness, not representations of individual people grounded in a particular situa-tion, time and place. To establish otherwise the first reference must be to the experience of actors who have tried to use this dialogue as a base for creating the persons in the play: are they able to create 'characters' which have credible and sustainable life? Unfortunately the evidence here is more than usually equivocal, because *The White Devil* is not an easy or straightforward play to perform; there is no common consensus on how to proceed, to the degree that there is about Shakespeare. Actors find Webster's dialogue hard to digest, requiring a very special kind of study and rehearsal. That done, the next obvious problem is to find a pace for performance which allows an audience to follow and understand all that is said. Put in another way, the difficulty is to give to the characters minds that are suffi-ciently adventurous, neither slowed down by the effort of compli-cated speech nor slurred or inaccurate in the moment-by-moment decisions which are necessary for perfomance. The next problem is to vary their physical beings sufficiently, and with sufficient speed, so that they can adapt to the varying engagement required by the dialogue. Here there is some indication that the original cast of the play experienced much the same trouble as actors today; for Bracciano's crazed death-scene Webster added an unusual stage-direction: '*These speeches are several kinds of distractions and in the action should appear so*' (V.iii.83.1–2). However 'the action' is to be understood—gesture, posture, activity, movement; acting in general: probably all are implied—the general message is that physical enactment must be at one with the words spoken. This is very conventional advice, but Webster thought that it needed to be re-stated in this context. In his end-note to the printed text, he did not say that his friend Richard Perkins should be particularly remembered for his speaking of the lines or his interpretation of his part; it was 'the worth of his *action*' that crowned both the beginning and the end of the play. For all his highly literate and ambitious verbal style and the nervous actuality it gives to speech, Webster has not written a literary tragedy. His characters should not be played as talking heads ventriloquized by the poet but as persons fully alive moment by moment in their inner consciousnesses and in their physical action within the interplay of performance.

From a consideration of verbal style and performance, the argument about Webster's worth must turn back again to the nature of his characterization. Is *The White Devil* peopled with ciphers convenient to an author's mind which is tortuously fixed on ingenious speech or on shock and sensation? Or are they persons whom the audience can recognize as people like themselves? Are they simplifications or exaggerations of such people, fashioned for their entertainment? Are they made up of shreds and patches, invented to puzzle or impress their audience? To what extent and in what ways can Vittoria, Flamineo, Bracciano, Francisco, Monticelso be called 'real'? Or do they represent ideas, types of persons, or elements within society?

Again certain warnings to the critics are embedded in the text, as if placed there to answer immediate adverse comment. Lodovico tells us that he is very ready to believe that a newly crowned pope has spoken words that are entirely different from his true message and intent:

> O the art,
> The modest form of greatness! that do sit
> Like brides at wedding dinners, with their looks turned
> From the least wanton jests, their puling stomach
> Sick of the modesty, when their thoughts are loose,
> Even acting of those hot and lustful sports
> Are to ensue about midnight . . .   (IV.iii.143–9)

Flamineo also tells us we may misjudge the most confident appearance or speech:

> I have lived
> Riotously ill, like some that live in court;
> And sometimes, when my face was full of smiles,
> Have felt the maze of conscience in my breast.
> Oft gay and honoured robes those tortures try;
> We think caged birds sing, when indeed they cry.   (V.iv.119–24)

Impressions, these speeches tell us, are not to be trusted, and they are not permanent; what a person seems to be at one moment is not necessarily what he or she is or will be a moment later. Flamineo talks readily about his 'varying of shapes' (IV.ii.248) and yet Francisco's disguise as Mulinassar fools everyone in accordance with a very ordinary theatrical convention. The contrasting appearances of Vittoria on her six entrances to the play have already been noticed here, and recent feminist critics have shown how she is governed both by what men say of her and by what she, independently, wills herself to be. Ignoring that she had suggested the murder of Camillo and Isabella, she tells Monticelso in the trial scene that

> For your names
> Of whore and murd'ress, they proceed from you,
> As if a man should spit against the wind,
> The filth returns in's face.   (III.ii.148–51)

When 'all the world speaks ill' of her, she wills it to be otherwise:

> No matter.
> I'll live so now I'll make that world recant
> And change her speeches.   (IV.ii.102–4)

Monticelso describes what most men and women have perceived Vittoria to be:

> Who knows not how, when several night by night
> Her gates were choked with coaches, and her rooms
> Outbraved the stars with several kind of lights,
> When she did counterfeit a prince's court
> In music, banquets and most riotous surfeits?   (III.ii.72–6)

But at certain moments, she speaks like a highly conventional woman. When her mother surprises her with Bracciano, she vows:

> I do protest if any chaste denial,
> If anything but blood could have allayed
> His long suit to me . . .   (I.ii.292–4)

She is almost certainly kneeling now, as Cornelia's following words suggest. Then a moment later she leaves the stage so precipitously that Bracciano does not allow her to be brought back; like an erring daughter, she now cries out, 'O me accurst'. When Bracciano is dying he calls for her, without apology or any apparent irony, saying: 'Where's this good woman? Had I infinite worlds / They were too little for thee' (V.iii.17–18). For the moment he may believe that epithet.

From time to time, and frequently at some particular climaxes, the characters speak almost proverbially, in set form expressing general truths. Webster's use of these '*sententiae*' has often been criticized as introducing more complacent or more naive statements than suit the progress of the drama. For example: 'My lord, supply your promises with deeds; / You know that painted meat no hunger feeds' (IV.ii.203–4). The rhyming conclusion hardly seems worth saying. Vittoria's last words, already quoted, cannot be received as the concluding and comprehensive expression of idiosyncratic character; at best they represent a facet of Vittoria's mind which comes unexpectedly to the fore at this point. She has been presented so variously that no one can be sure what these words mean to the speaker, how deeply the thought expressed has registered.

However on some occasions, especially when under pressure or in exultation, Webster's characters speak as if they needed to express the most obvious or the most reliable of their thoughts, puny though the ideas expressed may seem. Such a technique may be best under-stood as part of the presentation of an inner 'maze of conscience' and also of a will towards security which seems to be present somewhere in the minds of the bravest and most dangerous charac-ters. When Francisco sees Bracciano leaving the stage and knows that, by his own order, the helmet his victim has just put on is poisoned, the words he speaks are so unexpected that they seem to come from someone else; if they are intended to be ironic, that edge is not evenly present: 'He calls for his destruction. Noble youth, / I pity thy sad fate. Now to the barriers' (V.ii.81–2). In another writer, this might well be a lapse, a failure to imagine the experience of one specific character in a complicated scene; but with Webster strange shifts of tone and judgement seem to be an essential part of his dialogue's credibility.

STRUCTURE

These attitudes in a writer towards persons and speech affect the construction of the whole play, and to understand them a critic must consider more than dialogue and characterization. The working out of the consequences of a character's action, so that the conclusion expresses virtue or its opposite 'fully, whether true, / Or else adulterate', may indeed be one of the principles on which Webster formed and built his whole play. Perhaps he shared with Greek tragedians the notion that humankind learns through suffering, but the effect achieved seems too obscure, or too ambiguous, to satisfy an audience or account for the dramatist's purpose; besides it is effective only at isolated moments. A critical assessment of Webster's achievement in *The White Devil* must take into account the play's structure, narrative and character development.

Some comparatively minor characters have indeed been provided with a slow unfolding of their true natures. At first, Isabella de Medici, Francisco's sister and Bracciano's first wife, seems intent on 'mild entreaty' of her straying husband, eager not to cause louder quarrels and very willing to pardon any wrongs. Alone with him, she starts by protesting her devotion, but when Bracciano questions her meaning she introduces a string of innuendos that precipitates a quarrel almost as if that were her intention. She offers a peaceful separation, but only in a way which allows her to express a powerful sense of outrage that she has hidden until this moment. The transformation is so shocking, that now her own brother calls her 'a foolish, mad, / And jealous woman' (II.i.264–5). By the time she has finished, he is ready to laugh at her, and probably does (see ll. 274–6). The wife who had seemed to want only reconciliation now wishes she 'were a man' with power to whip her adversary (ll. 11 and 243–5). But Webster has still one more revelation to make, for her last lines express grief and heartbreak, even though she contains her feeling within a proverbial commonplace (see ll. 277–8). The way this woman has been treated by man makes her long passionately to be as cruel as if she were a man; and this is, or may be, against her innermost, truest nature.

Cornelia, as she interrupts her daughter and Bracciano in the second scene of the play, seems a very simple character, motivated entirely by her sense of family honour. At this moment, when the powerful duke is promising Vittoria everything he possesses, Cornelia foretells the 'fall' of her family. Left alone with Flamineo, she asks: 'What? Because we are poor, / Shall we be vicious?' and wishes 'O that I ne'er had borne thee' (I.ii.315–16, 334). But another change comes silently and swiftly, when at the beginning of Act V she appears at the marriage of Vittoria and Bracciano; like everyone else, she has forgotten morality and is drawn to the good fortune and precarious success which her children have achieved by the very means she had previously denounced. Later, after Flamineo has murdered his brother, Marcello, she lies to try to hide his guilt and so save his life. Then, as she prepares Marcello's corpse for burial, she goes mad: and again she changes, becoming childlike and addressing everyone on stage as 'all good people'. In her last moments, what she says and sings is full of sweetness, gentleness and compassion. As this new self is revealed, she is heard in total silence, piercing even Flamineo's hardened self-assurance (see V.iv.114–16).

Other minor characters change during the course of the play in still more provocative ways. When Camillo, Vittoria's cuckolded husband, is sent with Marcello to fight against the pirates at sea, he is at first fearful but then turns into a swaggering braggart: 'a'th'captain's humour right— / I am resolvèd to be drunk this night' (II.i.373–4). He is then seen, in dumb show, in the company of five other captains as '*they drink healths and dance*' (II.ii.37.3). His final action before being murdered is exercising on a vaulting horse—a strange ending for a man who has appeared so weak in the previous act. Were it not that Webster reveals unforeseen aspects of other characters, this might be regarded as a lapse in continuity or a manipulation of character for the sake of bringing off a trick in the plotting of the play.

The most spectacular change is in Cardinal Monticelso, Camillo's uncle. At first he is shown as an expert and secret manipulator, willing to 'play' with the life of his kinsman (II.i.391–4) and having a 'black book' with the names of murderers and other criminals who are available for his use (IV.i.1–76). When he is elected Pope, he excommunicates Bracciano and Vittoria, and so uses his new holy office to serve private revenge. But then Webster brings him back on stage to argue with Lodovico against taking Francisco's commission to revenge Isabella's death, and by the way to break the secrecy of a confession: after this *volte face*, he leaves the stage for the last time (IV.iii.116–27). Here Webster may show not a character revealing at last his own true nature but one serving his own personal ends by assuming a new outward behaviour in order to be more secure in his newly acquired office.

Uncertainty, fear, grief, compassion, an instinct towards laughter or unreflective courage: Webster draws on all these motives for characters to spring surprises and present new facets or new levels of their natures. Yet this technique which can clarify minor characters only renders the main persons of the drama more confusing and unknowable. Changes are so frequent, and so strange that it becomes difficult to see a progressive revelation of inward truth as a principle of its dramatic construction.

One of the main strands of the play's story is revenge, which in other tragedies of the time provided a clear theme and a narrative structure culminating in a major 'showdown' for all leading characters: *Hamlet* is the prime example. For *The White Devil*, however, Webster did not utilize these advantages of the revenge genre. He has no one revenger to order events and die at the end more or less vindicated by the wild justice he has forced on others. Monticelso's revenge for Camillo's death stops suddenly in Act IV. Francisco's for Isabella is carried out by others, first on Bracciano and then on Vittoria and Flamineo. Throughout Act V his presence in disguise is marginal, both in operation and in impact upon his victims. After the murder of Bracciano, as he and Lodovico look forward to the next stage of their revenge, he disclaims any moral purpose: 'Tush for justice. / What harms it justice?'; it is 'fame' alone that shall 'crown' his enterprise and 'quit the shame' (V.iii.268–71). A short penultimate scene (V.v) shows him acquiescing when Lodovico insists that he should leave the city before the last murders are attempted. In the final scene Lodovico, the chief instrument of revenge, might have become the point of moral focus, but he seems more concerned to retaliate for a blow Flamineo had once given him (see V.vi.190–4), or to know what he and Vittoria are thinking (see ll. 201, 221–2) , or to wish for more victims to 'feed / The famine of our vengeance' (ll. 198–201), than he is to make known the moral grounds for his actions. His concluding words are not of judgement but pride: 'I limbed this night-piece and it was my best' (l. 297). He has achieved a more glorious and more ingenious deed than those 'certain murders... / Bloody and full of horror' which he had committed previously and dismissed as mere 'flea-bitings' (I.i.31–2).

All the true surprises in the last scene—the business of Flamineo's false death and his sister's spitefulness, Zanche's sudden courage and loyalty, Flamineo's praise of Vittoria's nobleness and recognition of his own uncertainty and isolation, his call for thunder and Vittoria's talk of her storm-driven soul and of the happiness of those who have not lived among great men—these are what take and hold attention. They are not the marks of a revenge tragedy dominated by a single-minded revenger which is now drawing towards an inevi-

table and moral conclusion in the deaths of wrongdoers and a
salutary cleansing of the state.

Critics who look to characterization to explain the progress and
structure of the play find Webster's handling of Vittoria its most
recalcitrant element. Francisco, Bracciano, Monticelso, Flamineo
and Lodovico can all be seen as politicians, manipulators and
passionate men who come to distinctive ends; if not wholly known
by the audience, they are at least more fully known than at the
beginning, even though no one impression crowns all. Vittoria,
however, is different. She may be said to die nobly—or so Flamineo
asserts a little before the end—but it is not clear how she does this,
or to what effect on herself or on her audience. The biggest puzzle
is: 'O my greatest sin lay in my blood. / Now my blood pays for't'
(V.vi.240–1). Some critics take this as an acknowledgement of the
sin of her adultery, the 'blood' of the first line standing for sexual
desire. Some argue that she is speaking of an original sin, one
inherent in the life-blood of her humanity. Yet others take this
speech as a defiant acknowledgement that what she has done was
what she was born to do, or what her most vital instincts have
dictated. This crucial speech is capable of numerous interpretations,
and reader, actor or audience must choose how to interpret it—so
modifying the moral force of the entire play. This challenge is placed
where it cannot be ignored.

If characterization and moral judgements do not point to an
overriding purpose and cumulative structure for this play, and if
comparison with other revenge tragedies only makes Webster's purpose seem the more uncertain, is there any organizing principle
behind the writing other than an exploration of the nature of court
life, that mingling of personal ambition and power over others which
was at the centre of the land and responsible for its government? Has
this 'outing' procedure so taken precedence in Webster's mind that
he allowed the play to evolve from its Italian sources so that it
sprawls wherever his invention and his investigations nearer home
lead him?

It is tempting to answer that question in the affirmative and let the
matter rest, so that *The White Devil* can be accepted as a play written
before Webster was able to control his material more satisfactorily in
The Duchess of Malfi. In this tragedy, which followed only a few years
later, Bosola is a much stronger revenger in its last scene, crying out
unambiguously for moral judgment (see especially *Malfi*, V.v.81–7).
The later tragedy has its share of ambiguity, but its conclusion rings

with the conviction and moral purpose which are conspicuously lacking in *The White Devil*. In his first tragedy might Webster have been intent on mystification and avoidance? For example, by bringing Francisco to Bracciano's palace at Padua, against the evidence of all his sources, he did not materially strengthen the revenge theme as he might have done. He also invented Francisco's disguise as Mulinassar the Moor so that, in Lodovico's words, he 'most ridiculously' engages himself (V.v.2) and gets comically involved with Vittoria's maidservant, Zanche the Moor, in a subsidiary plot that does not materially alter anything. Webster also complicated the audience's view by introducing, against all narrative necessity or economy, the business of Flamineo's false death by unloaded pistols, with the occasion this gives for Vittoria, seconded by Zanche, to be possessed with an exultant or fearful vindictiveness: 'I tread the fire out / That would have been my ruin' (V.vi.124–5). This curious elaboration, at a moment of great tension arising from the story already in progress, occupies 167 lines of a total of 301 in the last scene. Critics tend to ignore the whole incident and it remains an unanswered challenge to most accounts of the structure and unity of *The White Devil*.

Is this play seriously flawed? Is it overwritten and uncertain in tone, a collection of incidents around a narrative which is much more complicated than it need have been? Or as its action advances through self-made obstacles and by-ways, can some organizing principle be sensed that was more important to its author than the manifestation of individual character? The most comprehensive answer to these questions may be that the play achieves a double view and that interplay between them was essential to Webster's purpose. While the court world is shown for the tangled web of ambition, lust, jealousy, cunning and violence, he also wanted to show the 'maze of conscience' (V.iv.122), the 'mist' that threatens self-knowledge in those who 'look up to heaven' (V.vi.259–60), and the hardening or the softening of feelings in those who survive in this world. His subject would thus be both political and psychological, and by pursuing the two issues he would show how any life was lived, rather than create clearly perceived exemplars of evil, virtue, truth or, perhaps, 'integrity'. The white devil herself is at the centre of the story and its staging, but she is by no means a stabilizing factor; she is always changing, and changing the audience's view of other persons.

We may conclude therefore that the play's structure has been

conceived intellectually, and that the whole is an expression of its
author's own consciousness. If we look beyond individual moments
or characters, we can often sense the construction lines linking
scenes and sequence of scenes; they show how Webster has manipu-
lated his material and controlled his imagination. For example, the
various aspects of the white devil are identified by a schematic and
symbolic use of colours. She is dressed at first in gold and perhaps
in scarlet or other vivid colours (see II.i.55 and III.ii.119–23); for Act
IV, in the House of Convertites, she wears the neutral colours of the
poor and penitent; and then, for Act V and her marriage, she
appears in bridal white. In the last scene, she is in widow's black, but
then, as she cries 'Behold my breast' (l. 216), she shows her white
skin; and moments later that is stained by blood from her wound,
unambiguously red. Such colour symbolism links together other
branches of the narrative: Zanche meets death claiming that her
blood is 'as red as either of theirs' (ll. 227–8); Francisco blackens his
face for disguise; at the end of the trial scene, Bracciano's son,
Giovanni, is dressed totally in black (see III.ii.310–13) and he may
remain so until the last moments of the play when he must represent
the future of the dukedom.

The change of colour in Monticelso's clothes is the most spectacular example of a visual symbolism holding the play together.
The complicated business of his election to the papacy, introduced
by Webster as if he had all the time in the world to indulge a taste
for pageantry, means that the cardinal's scarlet robes are removed
off-stage so that he reappears in the immaculate white vestments of
his elected office. His first action in this new guise is to pronounce
a blessing and forgiveness of sins, with an authority derived from
Christ. This tableau, purposefully held on stage by Webster, questions the use of the church's authority and the nature of retribution
and forgiveness. Only minutes later a second totally silent tableau,
part of a '*passage over the stage*', represents the marriage of Bracciano
and Vittoria (V.i.0.1). They have taken the sacrament of holy
matrimony: she also is dressed in white, and accompanied by the
mother who had cursed her in Act I. Besides, as the dialogue
subsequently makes clear (see V.i.57–61), the bridal couple are
accompanied by the same ambassadors who had filled the central
scene of 'The Arraignment of Vittoria' (III.ii.0.1) and that of the
Pope's election. After the latter, the actors playing the ambassadors
would have no time to change costumes, so they will be dressed in
robes displaying the symbols of Christ's passion and the Virgin

Mary's chastity and regality, as required by the dialogue to describe their 'habits' in IV.iii. So the silent *white* devil awakens visual echoes across the play, re-defining herself and others.

Colour symbolism was but one of the connections which Webster established between the various elements of his play so that it has a spatial and visual coherence, as well as a temporal one based on narrative lines. Not all its incidents are organized around a central journey or action leading to a climactic conclusion. The organization may be called mannerist or baroque, rather than medieval or renaissance. For example, several of the 'structural laws' of 'mannerist' art, as defined by Wylie Sypher in *Four Stages of Renaissance Style* (1955), apply well to *The White Devil*: 'diagonal or mobile point of view, disproportion, imbalance, thwarted verticality, funnel space, double functioning of members, contraction of materials, excess within rigid boundaries, shifting levels of statement, uncertain intervals, and tensions that [are] accommodated rather than resolved' (p. 184). Baroque, mannerist, or a mixture of several styles in the visual arts of the time in Europe provide some help in considering the structure which Webster created for *The White Devil*.

The White Devil was not divided into acts in its first edition, but editors agree that it was written in this form and about how it should be divided, even though the fifth act is about twice the length of any other. Webster's treatment of his theme demanded this disproportion; its focus opens out, rather than closes in, as the story draws to its close. Episodes and characters have been given multiple functions, so that they tend to develop in several directions. Towards the end, this begins to give an impression that only part of what the story implies has been shown, so that even then an audience is prompted to search beyond what is most obvious and straightforward. What has happened to Monticelso? What did Isabella mean to Lodovico? Who are the other conspirators? Why does Francisco choose to disguise himself as he does, and why is he in Padua? Who is now in charge of Giovanni, and what will his relationship be to Francisco? Why does Bracciano's ghost appear to Flamineo (he does not call for revenge), and how mad was he when he died? Above all, what is Vittoria thinking and doing (it is not certain that she is 'at her prayers', as Flamineo says), and how does she die?

Excess of incident and suggestion is held in check less by the five-act structure than by a system of contrasts and comparisons which ensure that one element will reflect on others and still further set the audience thinking. This structural device is most evident in episodes which could easily be cut in performance because they do not advance the narrative. So at the end of III.ii, Lodovico and Flamineo talk together, two men dependent on others more powerful than themselves. So while Flamineo serves Bracciano as secretary and pander, Marcello serves Francisco honestly as a soldier; when this role changes after he has joined Bracciano in Act V for the wedding, rivalry between the two brothers leads to his death. Bracciano's madness, induced by pain and betrayal, contrasts with Cornelia's brought on by grief. Isabella's fury is echoed later by Vittoria's, and her appearance to Francisco after her death is echoed by Bracciano's appearance as a ghost to Flamineo. Zanche's frank promiscuity and final courage contrast with those of her mistress. Doctor and Lawyer are both crazed; the ambassadors are present at four different occasions, although by the end only the English has individual significance. A cardinal becomes Pope; courtiers become Franciscans, both churchmen and assassins. Almost any element in this play has a reflection elsewhere: the structure of the play is one of multiple mirrors, linked together and held up to political and individual existence. They show how one consciousness—the author's, not that of any of his characters—saw the working of the world of power, ambition and desire.

STAGE HISTORY

In its own time *The White Devil* achieved considerable success after its less than satisfactory opening. By 1631 Queen Henrietta's Men had revived it at the Phoenix in Drury Lane and by 1672 its text had been printed three more times. On 2 October 1661 Samuel Pepys, the diarist, took only the smallest pleasure in a Restoration revival by the King's Company—'Methinks a very poor play'—however he went back to see it two days later, and performances continued to be given at intervals until 1682. The play's success can seldom have been assured; at this time, it was said to be 'acted but now and then; yet being well performed [was] very satisfactory to the Town'. There is no sign of a new production until 1925 when the Renaissance Theatre Company performed it at the New Scala in London on 11 October 1925. Another revival followed in 1935, and after World War II, beginning with a 1947 production with Margaret Rawlings as Vittoria, it began to be produced with more frequency. In Britain the National Theatre has staged it twice, in 1969 and 1991, and during the last few decades, despite rising financial difficulties (it is an expensive play to mount), there have been numerous productions by subsidized regional theatres and adventurous touring companies; university productions are probably still more common. The play is staged not only to give leading actors the opportunity to play major roles; its subtle construction and visual power have made it a director's and designer's play, an opportunity to recreate Webster's world and fill the stage with the characters' interconnected lives. In North America productions have been less common, perhaps because the original and confident directors needed to respond to Webster's wide vision have there tended to work for independent companies insufficient in size or entirely committed to developing new works.

FURTHER READING

During the last few decades Webster's claims for attention have been established beyond question. As late as 1971, in *English Drama to 1710* (London: Sphere Books), Christopher Ricks could dismiss the plots, action, and characterization of Webster's plays as 'crude stuff', and theatre critics marvel why any company would wish to stage such plays—*The White Devil* in particular, since it contained no central character of acceptable morality or consistent moral sense. As more editions have been published in the 1960s, 1970s, and 1980s, each the product of a fresh and careful scrutiny of the entire text, the ground has shifted, and Webster's presentation of an entire world, of a divided and changing society, has begun to hold attention, rather than his poetry, style or creation of a few individual and more or less heroic characters.

But differences of opinion remain, as the Introduction to this edition shows. Dissension among the critics can be sampled in a number of anthologies, notably *John Webster*, in the Penguin Critical Anthologies series, edited by G. K. and S. K. Hunter (Harmondsworth: Penguin, 1969) and *Webster: 'The White Devil' and 'The Duchess of Malfi': A Casebook*, edited by R. V. Holdsworth (London: Macmillan, 1975). Both reprint previously published articles, whereas Brian Morris's *John Webster*, a Mermaid Critical Commentary (London: Ernest Benn, 1970), presents previously unpublished studies and is consequently more unequal and strangely varied. But all these collections were published too soon to represent the full range of present opinion.

The White Devil is usually studied alongside *The Duchess of Malfi*, its sister (or twin) tragedy, and so students of this play need to seek out general books on Webster. Travis Bogard's *The Tragic Satire of John Webster* (Berkeley and Los Angeles: University of California Press, 1955) was one of the first to look beyond plotting and characterization to account for the mixture of dramatic modes within the play. It has been complemented, but not superseded, by Jacqueline Pearson's commentary in *Tragedy and Tragicomedy in the Plays of John Webster* (Manchester: Manchester University Press, 1980). The most compendious book is more recent: Charles R. Forker's *Skull Beneath the Skin: The Achievement of John Webster* (Carbondale and Edwardsville: Southern Illinois University Press, 1986). While offering little independent judgement, this careful study is what it was intended to be: comprehensive, well-balanced, and up-to-date for its time. For this play, it offers detailed analyses of characters and themes which lead on to consideration of 'the aesthetics of chaos'. This book is also a convenient place to start an enquiry into the social background of Webster himself, his education and reading, and the play's continuing influence. An altogether lighter and more affordable book, almost as recent and covering some of the same ground, is M. C. Bradbrook's *John Webster: Citizen and Dramatist* (London: Weidenfeld & Nicolson, 1980); here a study of the play in its social context is attempted, but not fully developed.

Access to the story and background of the real-life Vittoria Accoramboni, the documentation on which Webster's imagination thrived, may be found in Gunnar Boklund's *The Sources of the White Devil*, originally published in Uppsala, Sweden, in 1957, but more accessible in its North American edition (Cambridge, Mass.: Harvard University Press, 1957). Webster's two main sources, together with extracts from the description of the election of Popes which was used by Webster, are reprinted as Appendices in the original Revels Plays edition (1960), and its Introduction gives an account of the source material and Webster's adaptation of it. For incidental borrowings from other writers, the most complete reference book is R. W. Dent's *John Webster's Borrowing* (Berkeley and Los Angeles: University of California Press, 1960); but a good deal of this information can be found in the Revels Plays annotations. So it is for textual matters: there is no fuller treatment yet published than the Revels Textual Introduction and collation, although an article by Anthony Hammond in *Studies in Bibliography*, 39 (1986) modifies a few details, chiefly by arguing that three and not two compositors worked on the Quarto.

Among recent critical books, Dena Goldberg's *Between Worlds: A Study of the Plays of John Webster* (Waterloo, Ontario: Wilfrid Laurier University Press, 1989) concentrates on political and social issues, presenting *The White Devil* as the first of four anti-establishment plays which questioned authority's officers and their judgements. Taking its title from *The White Devil*, Christina Luckyj's *A Winter's Snake: Dramatic Form in the Tragedies of John Webster* (Athens, Georgia: University of Georgia Press, 1989) argues, against long-standing indictments for faults of structure, that the dramatist was intent on developing an indiosyncratic 'multiple unity' in which parallels, contrasts, subplots and nonlinear development were the main factors. Much the same argument is found in an earlier book by Ralph Berry, *The Art of John Webster* (Oxford: Oxford University Press, 1972), which starts with a wide-ranging discussion of Webster as a baroque artist, but its commentary on *The White Devil* is in more conventional terms of character and punishment for evil. (Berry finds *The Duchess of Malfi* a far more satisfying tragedy.) Richard Cave's volume on both *The White Devil* and *The Duchess of Malfi* in the Text and Performance series (London: Macmillan, 1989) offers well-considered critiques of two notable productions.

Among more general books, Jonathan Dollimore's *Radical Tragedy: Religion, Ideology and Power in the Drama of Shakespeare and His Contemporaries* (Brighton: Harvester Press, 1983) devotes a whole section to *The White Devil*, identifying moments when the playwright seems to draw accepted beliefs into crisis and doubt. Dympna Callaghan's *Woman and Gender in Renaissance Tragedy* (Atlantic Highlands, N.J.: Humanities Press International, 1989) studies Vittoria, Zanche, and Isabella, along with other women in *Lear*, *Othello*, and *The Duchess of Malfi*, to show that 'gender opposition is probably the most significant dynamic of Renaissance tragedy'; Vittoria's loss of chastity and her death by a sword separate her from those ideal women who are 'the common stock of tragedy' in Jacobean England.

THE
WHITE DEVIL

TO THE READER

In publishing this tragedy, I do but challenge to myself that
liberty, which other men have ta'en before me; not that I affect
praise by it, for, *nos haec novimus esse nihil*, only since it was
acted, in so dull a time of winter, presented in so open and
black a theatre, that it wanted (that which is the only grace   5
and setting out of a tragedy) a full and understanding auditory; and that since that time I have noted, most of the people
that come to that playhouse resemble those ignorant asses
(who visiting stationers' shops their use is not to inquire for
good books, but new books) I present it to the general view   10
with this confidence:

> *Nec rhoncos metues, maligniorum,*
> *Nec scombris tunicas, dabis molestas.*

If it be objected this is no true dramatic poem, I shall easily
confess it,—*non potes in nugas dicere plura meas: ipse ego quam*   15
dixi,—willingly, and not ignorantly, in this kind have I faulted;
for should a man present to such an auditory the most sententious tragedy that ever was written, observing all the critical
laws, as height of style, and gravity of person, enrich it with
the sententious *Chorus*, and as it were lifen death, in the   20
passionate and weighty *Nuntius*; yet after all this divine
rapture, *O dura messorum ilia*, the breath that comes from
the uncapable multitude is able to poison it, and ere it be

---

1. *challenge to*] claim for.
3. nos . . . nihil] We know these things are nothing (Martial).
4. *open*] i.e. unroofed, not indoors like a 'private' theatre.
5. *black*] i.e. dark, because of short daylight hours in winter.
8. *that playhouse*] the Red Bull; see Introduction.
12–13.] You [the poet's book] will not be afraid of the sneers of the
malicious, nor be used for wrapping mackerel (Martial).
14. *true*] regular.
15–16. non . . . dixi] You cannot say more against my trifles than I have
said myself (Martial).
20. *lifen*] bring vividly to life.
21. *weighty*] forcible, serious.
Nuntius] messenger.
22. O . . . ilia] O strong stomachs of harvesters (Horace, alluding to
countrypeople's fondness for garlic).

acted, let the author resolve to fix to every scene, this of
Horace,   25

   —*Haec hodie porcis comedenda relinques.*

To those who report I was a long time in finishing this tragedy,
I confess I do not write with a goose-quill, winged with two
feathers, and if they will needs make it my fault, I must answer them with that of Euripides to Alcestides, a tragic writer: 30
Alcestides objecting that Euripides had only in three days
composed three verses, whereas himself had written three
hundred: 'Thou tell'st truth,' (quoth he) 'but here's the difference,—thine shall only be read for three days, whereas mine
shall continue three ages.'   35
   Detraction is the sworn friend to ignorance. For mine own
part I have ever truly cherished my good opinion of other
men's worthy labours, especially of that full and heightened
style of Master Chapman; the laboured and understanding
works of Master Jonson; the no less worthy composures of the   40
both worthily excellent Master Beaumont, and Master
Fletcher; and lastly (without wrong last to be named) the right
happy and copious industry of Master Shakespeare, Master
Dekker, and Master Heywood, wishing what I write may be
read by their light; protesting, that, in the strength of mine   45
own judgement, I know them so worthy, that though I rest
silent in my own work, yet to most of theirs I dare (without
flattery) fix that of Martial:
   —*non norunt, haec monumenta mori.*

26.] What you leave will be for the pigs to eat today (Horace).
28. *with a goose-quill*] i.e. foolishly imitative and repetitive.
32. *verses*] lines.
39. *understanding*] displaying intelligence (?).
47. *in*] with regard to.
49.] These monuments do not know how to die (comparing literature
with ruined tombs).

[DRAMATIS PERSONAE

MONTICELSO, *a Cardinal, later Pope* PAUL IV.

FRANCISCO de MEDICI, *Duke of Florence; in the last Act, disguised as* MULINASSAR, *a Moor.*

The Duke of BRACCIANO, *otherwise, Paulo Giordano Orsini; husband first of Isabella, and later of Vittoria.*

GIOVANNI, *his son by Isabella.*

Count LODOVICO, *sometimes known as Lodowick; in love with Isabella; later a conspirator in the pay of Francisco.*

CAMILLO, *first husband of Vittoria; nephew to Monticelso.*

ANTONELLI \ *friends to Lodovico; later conspirators in the pay of*
GASPARO ∫ *Francisco.*

CARLO \ *of Bracciano's household; in secret league with Francisco.*
PEDRO ∫

HORTENSIO, *of Bracciano's household.*

FLAMINEO, *secretary to Bracciano; brother to Vittoria.*

MARCELLO, *his younger brother; of Francisco's household.*

ARRAGON, *a Cardinal.*

JULIO, *a doctor.*

ISABELLA, *first wife of Bracciano; sister to Francisco.*

VITTORIA COROMBONA, *a Venetian lady; wife first of Camillo, and later of Bracciano.*

CORNELIA, *mother to Vittoria, Flamineo, and Marcello.*

ZANCHE, *a Moor; servant to Vittoria; in love first with Flamineo, and later with Francisco.*

Ambassadors; Courtiers; Officers and Guards; Attendants.

Conjuror; Chancellor, Register and Lawyers; Conclavist; Armourer; Physicians; Page.

Matron of the House of Convertites; Ladies.

SCENE: *Rome for the first four acts, Padua for the fifth.*]

The White Devil

[I. i]

Enter Count LODOVICO, ANTONELLI *and* GASPARO.

Lodovico. Banished?
Antonelli.   It grieved me much to hear the sentence.
Lodovico. Ha, ha, O Democritus thy gods
    That govern the whole world!—Courtly reward,
    And punishment! Fortune's a right whore.
    If she give aught, she deals it in small parcels,   5
    That she may take away all at one swoop.
    This 'tis to have great enemies, God quite them.
    Your wolf no longer seems to be a wolf
    Than when she's hungry.
Gasparo.   You term those enemies
    Are men of princely rank.
Lodovico.   O, I pray for them.   10
    The violent thunder is adored by those
    Are pashed in pieces by it.
Antonelli.   Come, my lord,

Title. *White Devil*] See proverb: 'the white devil is worse than the black';
also = hypocrite. On Webster's use of colour symbolism, see Introduction.
    I.i.2. *Democritus*] The Greek philosopher (born *c.* 460 B.C.) thought the
gods were invented to give reasons for beneficial and harmful events; so
desire for reward and fear of punishment might be said to 'govern the whole
world'.
    4. *Fortune's . . . whore*] improving on the proverb, 'Fortune is fickle'.
    5. *parcels*] portions, instalments.
    6. *swoop*] (1) stroke; (2) commercial deal.
    7. *quite*] reward, requite.
    8. *wolf*] i.e. predatory 'great' man.
    9. *Than*] except.
    11-12. Cf. V.vi.276.
    pashed] struck, smashed.

You are justly doomed; look but a little back
Into your former life: you have in three years
Ruined the noblest earldom—
Gasparo.   Your followers   15
Have swallowed you like mummia, and being sick
With such unnatural and horrid physic
Vomit you up i'th'kennel—
Antonelli.   All the damnable degrees
Of drinkings have you staggered through—one citizen
Is lord of two fair manors, called you master   20
Only for caviare.
Gasparo.   Those noblemen
Which were invited to your prodigal feasts,
Wherein the phoenix scarce could 'scape your throats,
Laugh at your misery, as fore-deeming you
An idle meteor which drawn forth the earth   25
Would be soon lost i'th'air.
Antonelli.   Jest upon you,
And say you were begotten in an earthquake,
You have ruined such fair lordships.
Lodovico.   Very good.—
This well goes with two buckets; I must tend
The pouring out of either.
Gasparo.   Worse than these,   30
You have acted certain murders here in Rome,

---

13. *doomed*] sentenced.
16. *mummia*] pitch (used in embalming, and so = embalmed flesh).
17. *physic*] medicine.
18. *kennel*] gutter.
21. *Only for caviare*] i.e. merely for supplying you with caviare (a new and very rare delicacy).
23. *the phoenix*] an almost impossible luxury; it was said that only one of these fabled birds was alive at any one time.
24. *fore-deeming*] judging ahead of time.
25. *idle*] chance, meaningless.
meteor] The sun was said to draw forth impurities from garbage and dead bodies in the form of vaporous exhalations, or meteors.
29–30. *This . . . either*] i.e. with two of you pointing out my problems (when one bucket is coming up full, the other is going down empty), my attention is required on both fronts.
31. *acted*] carried out, brought about.

Bloody and full of horror.
Lodovico.   'Las, they were flea-bitings.
  Why took they not my head then?
Gasparo.   O my lord,
  The law doth sometimes mediate, thinks it good
  Not ever to steep violent sins in blood.   35
  This gentle penance may both end your crimes,
  And in the example better these bad times.
Lodovico. So,—but I wonder then some great men 'scape
  This banishment. There's Paulo Giordano Orsini,
  The Duke of Bracciano, now lives in Rome,   40
  And by close pandarism seeks to prostitute
  The honour of Vittoria Corombona—
  Vittoria, she that might have got my pardon
  For one kiss to the duke.
Antonelli. Have a full man within you.   45
  We see that trees bear no such pleasant fruit
  There where they grew first as where they are new set.
  Perfumes the more they are chafed the more they render
  Their pleasing scents, and so affliction
  Expresseth virtue, fully, whether true,   50
  Or else adulterate.
Lodovico.   Leave your painted comforts.
  I'll make Italian cut-works in their guts
  If ever I return.
Gasparo.   O, sir.
Lodovico.   I am patient.
  I have seen some ready to be executed
  Give pleasant looks, and money, and grown familiar   55
  With the knave hangman, so do I,—I thank them,
  And would account them nobly merciful
  Would they dispatch me quickly.
Antonelli.   Fare you well.

---

34. *mediate*] avoid extremes, settle by mediation.
37. *in the example*] by means of its example.
41. *close*] secret.
45.] Be the complete, the fully fortified and resolved man.
47. *new set*] transplanted.
51. *painted*] false.
52. *cut-works*] openwork embroidery.

We shall find time I doubt not to repeal
        Your banishment.
Lodovico.   I am ever bound to you.   60
                                A sennet sounds.
        This is the world's alms—pray make use of it—
        Great men sell sheep, thus to be cut in pieces,
        When first they have shorn them bare and sold their
                fleeces.   *Exeunt.*

[I. ii]

            Enter BRACCIANO, CAMILLO, FLAMINEO, VITTORIA
                    COROMBONA[, *and* Attendants].

Bracciano. Your best of rest.
Vittoria.   Unto my lord the duke,
        The best of welcome. More lights! Attend the duke.
                            [*Exeunt* CAMILLO and VITTORIA.]
Bracciano. Flamineo.
Flamineo.   My lord?
Bracciano.   Quite lost, Flamineo.
Flamineo. Pursue your noble wishes; I am prompt
        As lightning to your service,—O my lord!   5
        (*Whispers*) The fair Vittoria, my happy sister
        Shall give you present audience.—Gentlemen,
        Let the caroche go on, and 'tis his pleasure
        You put out all your torches and depart.
                                [*Exeunt* Attendants.]
Bracciano. Are we so happy?
Flamineo.   Can't be otherwise?   10
        Observed you not tonight, my honoured lord,
        Which way soe'er you went she threw her eyes?

60.S.D. sennet] flourish of trumpets, accompanying a ceremonial
entrance.
61. *This*] i.e. the following maxim.
make . . . it] profit by the knowledge.

I.ii.0.1.] The location is Camillo's house.
1. *Your . . . rest*] Sleep well.
7. *Shall . . . audience*] will receive you immediately.
8. *caroche*] a stately kind of coach.

I have dealt already with her chamber-maid
Zanche the Moor, and she is wondrous proud
To be the agent for so high a spirit.　　　　　　　　　　　　15
Bracciano. We are happy above thought, because 'bove merit.
Flamineo. 'Bove merit! We may now talk freely. 'Bove merit;
　　what is't you doubt? Her coyness? That's but the
　　superficies of lust most women have; yet why should
　　ladies blush to hear that named, which they do not fear to　　20
　　handle? O, they are politic; they know our desire is in-
　　creased by the difficulty of enjoying, whereas satiety is a
　　blunt, weary and drowsy passion. If the buttery-hatch at
　　court stood continually open, there would be nothing so
　　passionate crowding, nor hot suit after the beverage,—　　25
Bracciano. O, but her jealous husband.
Flamineo. Hang him, a gilder that hath his brains perished
　　with quicksilver is not more cold in the liver. The great
　　barriers moulted not more feathers than he hath shed
　　hairs, by the confession of his doctor. An Irish gamester　　30
　　that will play himself naked, and then wage all downward
　　at hazard, is not more venturous. So unable to please a

---

　　19. *superficies*] outward (false) appearance.
　　21. *handle*] (1) touch; (2) talk about.
　　politic] cunning.
　　23. *buttery-hatch*] half-door over which provisions and drink were served
from the storeroom.
　　25. *hot suit after*] urgent request for.
　　27–8. *gilder . . . quicksilver*] In gilding, an amalgam of gold and mercury
was applied to the object and then the mercury (*quicksilver*) abstracted as a
vapour by the application of heat; through inhaling this poisonous vapour,
gilders were prone to tremors and insanity.
　　28. *liver*] the supposed seat of the passions.
　　29. *barriers*] For entertainment and display of prowess, duels were
fought on foot across a waist-high barrier; the usual weapons were pike and
sword.
　　feathers] plumes struck from the combatants' helmets.
　　29–30. *shed hairs*] implying either lack of virility or that he has been treated
for venereal disease. Hair loss is also a sign of old age, but Camillo is stupid,
weak, and 'unable to please a woman', rather than old; he is young enough
to join Marcello and other soldiers in drinking, dancing and gymnastics (see
II.ii.37.1ff.).
　　31. *play . . . naked*] lose all he stands up in at the gaming tables.
　　all downward] i.e. hair, toenails, testicles—everything that can be cut off.
　　32. *venturous*] i.e. Camillo is ready to wage his virility because he has none.

woman that like a Dutch doublet all his back is shrunk
into his breeches.

Shroud you within this closet, good my lord,—   35
Some trick now must be thought on to divide
My brother-in-law from his fair bed-fellow,—

Bracciano. O, should she fail to come,—

Flamineo. I must not have your lordship thus unwisely amorous. I myself have loved a lady and pursued her with a   40
great deal of under-age protestation, whom some three or
four gallants that have enjoyed would with all their hearts
have been glad to have been rid of. 'Tis just like a summer
bird-cage in a garden: the birds that are without despair
to get in, and the birds that are within despair and are in   45
a consumption for fear they shall never get out. Away,
away, my lord,—

                              [*Exit* BRACCIANO.]

                      Enter CAMILLO.

[*Aside*] See, here he comes. This fellow by his apparel
Some men would judge a politician,
But call his wit in question you shall find it   50
Merely an ass in's foot-cloth. [*To Camillo*] How now,
        brother—
What, travailing to bed to your kind wife?

Camillo. I assure you brother, no. My voyage lies
More northerly, in a far colder clime,—
I do not well remember, I protest,   55
When I last lay with her.

Flamineo. Strange you should lose your count.

Camillo. We never lay together but ere morning

---

33. *Dutch doublet*] a fashion for tight-fitting doublets worn with large,
stuffed-out breeches.

  back] a weak back is another sign of impotency.

  41. *under-age protestation*] youthful, inexperienced wooing.

  51. *foot-cloth*] a rich cloth laid over a horse's back to protect its rider from
mud and dust, a mark of dignity and rank; Camillo's clothes are rich, but
underneath he has the mind of an ass.

  52. *travailing*] (1) journeying; (2) working, struggling (with a suggestion
that sex is hard work for Camillo).

  57. *count*] (1) numbering; (2) the female pudenda.

  58. *but*] except.

       There grew a flaw between us.
Flamineo.   'Thad been your part
       To have made up that flaw.
Camillo.   True, but she loathes   60
       I should be seen in't.
Flamineo.   Why sir, what's the matter?
Camillo. The duke your master visits me—I thank him,
       And I perceive how like an earnest bowler
       He very passionately leans that way
       He should have his bowl run—
Flamineo.   I hope you do not think—   65
Camillo. That noblemen bowl booty? Faith his cheek
       Hath a most excellent bias; it would fain
       Jump with my mistress.
Flamineo.   Will you be an ass,
       Despite your Aristotle, or a cuckold
       Contrary to your ephemerides   70
       Which shows you under what a smiling planet
       You were first swaddled?
Camillo.   Pew wew, sir, tell not me
       Of planets nor of ephemerides—
       A man may be made cuckold in the day-time
       When the stars' eyes are out.
Flamineo.   Sir, God boy you.   75
       I do commit you to your pitiful pillow

    59, 60. *flaw*] from *voyage* (l. 53) grows the idea of two ships which *lay together*, and then of a *flaw*, or squall, which parted them; Flamineo then turns the sense by using *flaw* as 'crack' or 'breach' (with bawdy reference to the female sexual anatomy).

    60. *made up*] fill up, supply deficiencies in (used here with sexual implications).

    66. *bowl booty*] two players combine to cheat a third.

    66–8. *cheek . . . mistress*] a sequence of bowling terms: Bracciano's cheek has an inclination, like that of the *bias* (or weight) in the *cheek* (or side) of a bowl, to come together with Vittoria's, as a bowl will *jump with* (or run up against) the *mistress* (or 'jack', the small white ball at which the bowls are aimed). There is also a quibble on *jump with* = 'lie with'.

    69. *Despite your Aristotle*] illogically, despite your philosophical learning.

    70. *ephemerides*] astronomical almanacs.

    75. *boy you*] a contracted form of 'be with you'.

Stuffed with horn-shavings.

Camillo.   Brother—

Flamineo.   God refuse me,
Might I advise you now, your only course
Were to lock up your wife.

Camillo.   'Twere very good.

Flamineo. Bar her the sight of revels.

Camillo.   Excellent.   80

Flamineo. Let her not go to church, but like a hound
In leon at your heels.

Camillo.   'Twere for her honour—

Flamineo. And so you should be certain in one fortnight,
Despite her chastity or innocence
To be cuckolded, which yet is in suspense.   85
This is my counsel and I ask no fee for't.

Camillo. Come, you know not where my night-cap wrings me.

Flamineo. Wear it a' th' old fashion, let your large ears come
through, it will be more easy. Nay, I will be bitter,—bar
your wife of her entertainment; women are more willingly   90
and more gloriously chaste when they are least restrained
of their liberty. It seems you would be a fine capricious
mathematically jealous coxcomb; take the height of your
own horns with a Jacob's staff afore they are up. These

---

77. *horn-shavings*] Horns were said to grow on a cuckold's forehead:
outrageously, Flamineo implies that Camillo has shaved his off and hidden
the shavings in his pillow.

81. *but*] unless.

82. *leon*] leash.

87. *wrings*] i.e. the cap is too small to hide his cuckold's horn.

88. *ears*] Flamineo pretends that Camillo meant to say that his cap had not
room enough to hide his ass's ears.

89–90. *bar . . . entertainment*] Flamineo speaks sarcastically: he mockingly
suggests that to keep Vittoria under lock and key will be to encourage her to
seek her pleasure with other men (see also ll. 81–5).

92. *capricious*] pun on Latin *caper*, the horned goat.

93. *mathematically*] scientifically precise.

coxcomb] fool (after the fool's bauble or sceptre, with phallic suggestion).

94. *Jacob's staff*] instrument for measuring altitudes (from a pilgrim's
staff as used on pilgrimage to the shrine of St James (Latin *Jacobus*) of
Compostella).

politic enclosures for paltry mutton makes more rebellion   95
in the flesh than all the provocative electuaries doctors
have uttered since last Jubilee.

Camillo. This doth not physic me.

Flamineo. It seems you are jealous. I'll show you the error of
it by a familiar example. I have seen a pair of spectacles   100
fashioned with such perspective art that, lay down but
one twelvepence a' th' board, 'twill appear as if there
were twenty. Now, should you wear a pair of these spectacles, and see your wife tying her shoe, you would
imagine twenty hands were taking up of your wife's   105
clothes, and this would put you into a horrible causeless
fury,—

Camillo. The fault there, sir, is not in the eye-sight—

Flamineo. True, but they that have the yellow jaundice think
all objects they look on to be yellow. Jealousy is worser: 110
her fits present to a man, like so many bubbles in a basin
of water, twenty several crabbed faces,—many times
makes his own shadow his cuckold-maker.

Enter [VITTORIA] COROMBONA.

See, she comes. What reason have you to be jealous of
this creature? What an ignorant ass or flattering knave   115
might he be counted, that should write sonnets to her
eyes, or call her brow the snow of Ida, or ivory of Corinth,

---

95. *politic*] crafty (with pun on 'politically motivated'; see *rebellion*).

mutton] loose women (slang); Flamineo compares incarcerating women to
the enclosures of common land for sheep farming that were causing hardship
in rural England.

96. *provocative*] exciting to lust, or to action.

electuaries] (1) medicines; (2) aphrodisiacs.

97. *uttered*] promoted, put on sale.

Jubilee] year instituted by the Pope, as a time for obtaining indulgences for
sin by acts of piety or beneficence; the most recent was in 1600.

98. *physic*] cure.

101. *perspective*] optical.

102. *board*] card, or gaming, table.

113. *shadow*] reflection, image.

117. *snow of Ida*] i.e. sheep's wool (a pure white complexion was considered beautiful); this range of mountains near Troy was famous not for
snow, but as a mythical pastoral retreat for shepherds, Paris among them.

Corinth] The Greek town had no particular connection with 'ivory', but

or compare her hair to the blackbird's bill, when 'tis liker
the blackbird's feather? This is all: be wise; I will make
you friends and you shall go to bed together. Marry,   120
look you, it shall not be your seeking; do you stand
upon that by any means. Walk you aloof; I would
not have you seen in't.—Sister (my lord attends you
in the banqueting-house), your husband is wondrous
discontented.   125

Vittoria. I did nothing to displease him; I carved to him at
suppertime—

Flamineo. (You need not have carved him, in faith, they say
he is a capon already,—I must now seemingly fall out
with you.) Shall a gentleman so well descended as   130
Camillo (a lousy slave that within this twenty years rode
with the black guard in the duke's carriage 'mongst spits
and dripping-pans)—

Camillo. Now he begins to tickle her.

Flamineo. An excellent scholar (one that hath a head filled   135
with calves' brains without any sage in them), come
crouching in the hams to you for a night's lodging?—(that
hath an itch in's hams, which like the fire at the glass-
house hath not gone out this seven years). Is he not a
courtly gentleman? (When he wears white satin one   140
would take him by his black muzzle to be no other creature than a maggot.) You are a goodly foil, I confess, well

---

was renowned as a market for rich goods and the beauty and number of its
prostitutes.

118. *compare . . . bill*] an ironically mundane allusion to the conventional
praise of a fair beauty.

121. *stand*] insist.

123–44.] The passages in parentheses are asides to Vittoria.

126. *carved*] (1) served (at table); (2) showed courtesy, made advances.

129. *capon*] castrated rooster, eunuch.

132. *black guard*] lowest menials of a noble household.

134. *tickle*] arouse, provoke.

136. *sage*] (1) herb used in cooking; (2) sagacity (a 'calf' = young fool).

138–9. *glass-house*] glass factory.

140–2. *When . . . maggot*] i.e. his dark head on top of a smart white body
makes Camillo look like a *maggot*.

142. *foil*] setting for a jewel.

set out (but covered with a false stone—yon counterfeit
diamond).

Camillo. He will make her know what is in me.   145

Flamineo. [*Aside to Vittoria*] Come, my lord attends you; thou
shalt go to bed to my lord.

Camillo. Now he comes to't.

Flamineo. With a relish as curious as a vintner going to taste
new wine.—[*To Camillo*] I am opening your case hard.   150

Camillo. A virtuous brother, a'my credit.

Flamineo. He will give thee a ring with a philosopher's stone
in it.

Camillo. Indeed, I am studying alchemy.

Flamineo. Thou shalt lie in a bed stuffed with turtles' feathers, 155
swoon in perfumed linen like the fellow was smothered in
roses. So perfect shall be thy happiness, that as men at sea
think land and trees and ships go that way they go, so
both heaven and earth shall seem to go your voyage. Shalt
meet him, 'tis fixed, with nails of diamonds to inevitable   160
necessity.

Vittoria. [*Aside to Flamineo*] How shall's rid him hence?

Flamineo. [*Aside to Vittoria*] I will put breese in's tail, set him
gadding presently.—[*To Camillo*] I have almost wrought
her to it,—I find her coming, but—might I advise you   165
now—for this night I would not lie with her, I would cross
her humour to make her more humble.

Camillo. Shall I, shall I?

Flamineo. It will show in you a supremacy of judgement.

---

143. *covered*] sexual pun; a stallion is said to 'cover' a mare.

150. *opening your case*] (1) pleading your case; (2) preparing for your sexual
entry; *hard* may also play on sexual meaning.

151. *a'my credit*] on my word, by my faith.

152. *philosopher's stone*] the object of alchemists' search; it was reputed to
turn base metals into gold, prolong life and cure diseases.

160. *nails of diamonds*] an image of luxurious expense; such nails would
last for ever. The match, says Flamineo with mock eloquence, is made in
heaven.

162. *shall's*] shall we.

163. *breese*] gadflies.

164. *presently*] immediately, at once.

165. *coming*] forward, sexually aroused.

Camillo. True, and a mind differing from the tumultuary   170
    opinion, for *quae negata grata.*

Flamineo. Right—you are the adamant shall draw her to you,
    though you keep distance off:—

Camillo. A philosophical reason.

Flamineo. Walk by her a'the nobleman's fashion, and tell her   175
    you will lie with her at the end of the progress—

Camillo. Vittoria, I cannot be induced, or as a man would say
    incited—

Vittoria. To do what, sir?

Camillo. To lie with you tonight; your silkworm useth to fast   180
    every third day, and the next following spins the better.
    Tomorrow at night I am for you.

Vittoria. You'll spin a fair thread, trust to't.

Flamineo. But do you hear—I shall have you steal to her
    chamber about midnight.   185

Camillo. Do you think so? Why, look you, brother, because
    you shall not think I'll gull you, take the key, lock me into
    the chamber, and say you shall be sure of me.

Flamineo. In troth I will, I'll be your jailer once,—
    But have you ne'er a false door?   190

Camillo. A pox on't, as I am a Christian. Tell me tomorrow
    how scurvily she takes my unkind parting—

Flamineo. I will.

Camillo. Didst thou not mark the jest of the silkworm?
    Goodnight—in faith I will use this trick often,—   195

Flamineo. Do, do, do.

                                            Exit CAMILLO.

---

170. *tumultuary*] irregular, haphazard.

171. quae . . . grata] what is denied is desired (proverbial).

172. *adamant*] metal of great hardness (in fable), magnet.

174. *philosophical*] (1) wise; (2) scientific.

176. *progress*] Nobles were obliged to attend their king on long series of state visits.

177. *man*] Camillo is trying to boast of his manhood.

180-1. *silkworm . . . better*] In fact silkworms fast two days before they spin, and then spin for up to nine days without food.

useth] is accustomed.

183. *spin . . . thread*] be very clever (common proverb), here with mocking allusion to Camillo's poor performance as a lover.

192. *scurvily*] ill-temperedly, rudely.

unkind] (1) unnatural; (2) ungentle.

So, now you are safe. Ha ha ha, thou entanglest thyself in
thine own work like a silkworm—

Enter BRACCIANO.

Come sister, darkness hides your blush. Women are like
curst dogs: civility keeps them tied all daytime, but they   200
are let loose at midnight; then they do most good or most
mischief. My lord, my lord—
Bracciano. Give credit: I could wish time would stand still
And never end this interview, this hour,
But all delight doth itself soon'st devour.   205

> ZANCHE *brings out a carpet, spreads it and
> lays on it two fair cushions. Enter* CORNELIA
> [*listening, behind*].

Let me into your bosom, happy lady,
Pour out instead of eloquence my vows.—
Loose me not madam, for if you forgo me
I am lost eternally.
Vittoria.   Sir in the way of pity
I wish you heart-whole.
Bracciano.   You are a sweet physician.
Vittoria. Sure, sir, a loathed cruelty in ladies   210
Is as to doctors many funerals;
It takes away their credit.
Bracciano.   Excellent creature!
We call the cruel fair; what name for you
That are so merciful?
Zanche.   See now they close.
Flamineo. Most happy union.   215
Cornelia. [*Aside*] My fears are fall'n upon me. O my heart!
My son the pandar. Now I find our house
Sinking to ruin. Earthquakes leave behind,

---

200. *curst*] (1) savage, vicious; (2) shrewish.
civility] sense of social rules, good manners.
203. *Give credit*] believe me.
208. *Loose*] (1) loose, withdraw hold over; (2) lose, destroy.
forgo] forsake, neglect.
209. *lost eternally*] damned, ruined.

Where they have tyrannized, iron, or lead, or stone, 220
But—woe to ruin—violent lust leaves none.
Bracciano. What value is this jewel?
Vittoria   'Tis the ornament
Of a weak fortune.
Bracciano. In sooth, I'll have it; nay I will but change
My jewel for your jewel.
Flamineo.   Excellent, 225
His jewel for her jewel.—Well put in, duke.
Bracciano. Nay, let me see you wear it.
Vittoria   Here, sir.
Bracciano. Nay, lower, you shall wear my jewel lower.
Flamineo. That's better—she must wear his jewel lower.
Vittoria. To pass away the time I'll tell your grace 230
A dream I had last night.
Bracciano.   Most wishedly.
Vittoria. A foolish idle dream,—
Methought I walked about the mid of night
Into a church-yard, where a goodly yew-tree
Spread her large root in ground. Under that yew, 235
As I sat sadly leaning on a grave,
Chequered with cross-sticks, there came stealing in
Your duchess and my husband; one of them
A pick-axe bore, th'other a rusty spade,
And in rough terms they gan to challenge me 240
About this yew.
Bracciano.   That tree.
Vittoria.   This harmless yew.
They told me my intent was to root up
That well-grown yew, and plant i'th'stead of it

222–9. *jewel*] wordplay, occasioned by a jewelled ornament which Vittoria
wears, allows talk of chastity, honour and body-parts; Flamineo's 'put in'
(l. 226) and 'lower' (l. 229) clinch its most physical meanings.

234–55. *yew*] The pun on 'you' is not fully explicit until Bracciano's
interpretation, l. 261; at times the association of a 'yew-tree' with mourning
and death is also close to the surface meaning (see, especially, 'sacred yew',
l. 255).

237. *cross-sticks*] a possible reference to witchcraft and, more prosaically,
to 'chequered' shade under the yew-tree.

A withered blackthorn, and for that they vowed
To bury me alive. My husband straight　　　　　　　　245
With pick-axe gan to dig, and your fell duchess
With shovel, like a Fury, voided out
The earth and scattered bones. Lord, how methought
I trembled, and yet for all this terror
I could not pray.　　　　　　　　　　　　　　　　250
Flamineo. No, the devil was in your dream.
Vittoria. When to my rescue there arose, methought,
A whirlwind, which let fall a massy arm
From that strong plant,
And both were struck dead by that sacred yew　　255
In that base shallow grave that was their due.
Flamineo. Excellent devil!
She hath taught him in a dream
To make away his duchess and her husband.
Bracciano. Sweetly shall I interpret this your dream.　260
You are lodged within his arms who shall protect you,
From all the fevers of a jealous husband,
From the poor envy of our phlegmatic duchess.
I'll seat you above law and above scandal,
Give to your thoughts the invention of delight　　265
And the fruition; nor shall government
Divide me from you longer than a care
To keep you great. You shall to me at once

---

244. *blackthorn*] Vittoria makes her dream doubly allusive: from Isabella and Camillo's perspective, Bracciano is the 'withered blackthorn'; but, in her own mind, Bracciano is the 'well-grown yew'. She leaves the two opposing interpretations unresolved and so prompts Bracciano to 'interpret' (l. 260).

246. *fell*] cruel, angry.

247. *Fury*] spirit of revenge.

voided] emptied.

253. *whirlwind*] in one possible interpretation, Cornelia; in another, the force of Bracciano's anger.

263. *envy*] ill-will, malice.

phlegmatic] an excess of phlegm, the watery humour, was said to be shown in a cold, dull temper.

264. *seat*] with the implication of being enthroned as duchess; Bracciano's 'great' and 'dukedom' also hint that he will marry Vittoria, making her an equal consort.

266. *government*] (1) discretion; (2) the duties of a prince.

Be dukedom, health, wife, children, friends and all.
Cornelia. [*Coming forward*] Woe to light hearts—they still
    forerun our fall.   270
Flamineo. What Fury raised thee up?—Away, away!
                                        Exit ZANCHE.
Cornelia. What make you here, my lord, this dead of night?
    Never dropt mildew on a flower here
    Till now.
Flamineo.   I pray, will you go to bed then,
    Lest you be blasted?
Cornelia.   O that this fair garden   275
    Had with all poisoned herbs of Thessaly
    At first been planted, made a nursery
    For witchcraft, rather than a burial plot
    For both your honours.
Vittoria.   Dearest mother, hear me.
Cornelia. O thou dost make my brow bend to the earth,   280
    Sooner than nature.—See the curse of children!
    In life they keep us frequently in tears,
    And in the cold grave leave us in pale fears.
Bracciano. Come, come, I will not hear you.
Vittoria.   Dear my lord.
Cornelia. Where is thy duchess now, adulterous duke?   285
    Thou little dreamed'st this night she is come to Rome.
Flamineo. How? Come to Rome?—
Vittoria.   The duchess,—
Bracciano.   She had been better,—
Cornelia. The lives of princes should like dials move,
    Whose regular example is so strong,
    They make the times by them go right or wrong.   290
Flamineo. So, have you done?
Cornelia.   Unfortunate Camillo.

---

271. *Away, away*] addressed to Zanche (who has been settled close to
Flamineo; see ll. 215–16) because he wants no witness or complication for
what is to follow; even he would not address his mother so unceremoniously.
   275. *blasted*] (1) blighted; (2) blown to pieces.
   276. *Thessaly*] a district in Greece, famed in antiquity for witchcraft and
poisonous drugs.
   282. *frequently*] incessantly.
   288. *dials*] sundials, clocks.
   290. *times*] (1) passage of time; (2) state of affairs at a particular period.

Vittoria. I do protest if any chaste denial,
    If anything but blood could have allayed
    His long suit to me,—
Cornelia.   I will join with thee,
    To the most woeful end e'er mother kneeled,—   295
    If thou dishonour thus thy husband's bed,
    Be thy life short as are the funeral tears
    In great men's,—
Bracciano.   Fie, fie, the woman's mad.
Cornelia. Be thy act Judas-like—betray in kissing.
    May'st thou be envied during his short breath,   300
    And pitied like a wretch after his death.
Vittoria. O me accurst!

                                  Exit VITTORIA.

Flamineo. Are you out of your wits, my lord?
    I'll fetch her back again.
Bracciano.   No I'll to bed.
    Send Doctor Julio to me presently.—   305
    Uncharitable woman, thy rash tongue
    Hath raised a fearful and prodigious storm.
    Be thou the cause of all ensuing harm.

                                Exit BRACCIANO.

Flamineo. Now, you that stand so much upon your honour,
    Is this a fitting time a'night, think you,   310
    To send a duke home without e'er a man?
    I would fain know where lies the mass of wealth
    Which you have hoarded for my maintenance,
    That I may bear my beard out of the level
    Of my lord's stirrup.
Cornelia.   What? Because we are poor,   315
    Shall we be vicious?
Flamineo.   Pray, what means have you

---

   293. *blood*] (1) life-blood; (2) passion, sensual appetite; (3) bloodshed. See also V.vi.240–1.
   294. *I . . . thee*] presumably Vittoria is already kneeling.
   298. *men's*] 'lives' should be inferred, from 'life' of l. 297.
   307. *prodigious*] ominous, portentous.
   311. *without . . . man*] unattended.
   314–15. *bear . . . stirrup*] i.e. cease to walk beside my lord's horse in a humble position.

To keep me from the galleys, or the gallows?
My father proved himself a gentleman,
Sold all's land, and like a fortunate fellow
Died ere the money was spent. You brought me up   320
At Padua, I confess, where I protest,
For want of means—the university judge me—
I have been fain to heel my tutor's stockings
At least seven years; conspiring with a beard
Made me a graduate; then to this duke's service.   325
I visited the court, whence I returned,
More courteous, more lecherous by far,
But not a suit the richer. And shall I,
Having a path so open and so free
To my preferment, still retain your milk   330
In my pale forehead? No, this face of mine
I'll arm and fortify with lusty wine
'Gainst shame and blushing.
Cornelia. O that I ne'er had borne thee,—
Flamineo.   So would I.
I would the common'st courtesan in Rome   335
Had been my mother rather than thyself.
Nature is very pitiful to whores
To give them but few children, yet those children
Plurality of fathers; they are sure
They shall not want. Go, go,   340
Complain unto my great lord cardinal;
Yet may be he will justify the act.
Lycurgus wond'red much men would provide

---

321. *Padua*] the most ancient and respected university in Italy.

323.] Poor scholars often kept themselves at university by working as servants for their college, richer fellow students or tutors.

324–5. *conspiring . . . graduate*] The exact sense is doubtful: Flamineo may mean that by growing up he completed the requirements for a degree; or he may imply the connivance of a very senior man for favours done, possibly involving sexual blackmail.

327. *courteous*] (1) well-mannered; (2) like a (corrupt) courtier.

328. *not . . . richer*] (1) no better dressed; (2) without having been granted any one request for self-promotion (see 'preferment', l. 330).

330–1. *milk . . . forehead*] being a mother's boy would cause Flamineo to have a cowardly, pale complexion.

343. *Lycurgus*] Athenian statesman and orator (*c.* 390–325 B.C.), an efficient financial adminstrator who denounced disloyalty and corruption; the source for his opinion about mares and wives is unknown.

Good stallions for their mares, and yet would suffer
Their fair wives to be barren.   345
Cornelia. Misery of miseries!

                          Exit CORNELIA.

Flamineo. The duchess come to court! I like not that.
We are engaged to mischief and must on.
As rivers to find out the ocean
Flow with crook bendings beneath forcèd banks,   350
Or as we see, to aspire some mountain's top,
The way ascends not straight, but imitates
The subtle foldings of a winter's snake,
So who knows policy and her true aspect,
Shall find her ways winding and indirect.   *Exit.*   355

[II. i]

    Enter FRANCISCO DE MEDICI, Cardinal MONTICELSO,
MARCELLO, ISABELLA, young GIOVANNI, *with* Attendants.

Francisco. Have you not seen your husband since you arrived?
Isabella. Not yet, sir.
Francisco.   Surely he is wondrous kind.
If I had such a dove-house as Camillo's
I would set fire on't, were't but to destroy
The pole-cats that haunt to't.—My sweet cousin!   5
Giovanni. Lord uncle, you did promise me a horse
And armour.
Francisco.   That I did, my pretty cousin.

---

350. *crook*] crooked.
forced] artificial, man-made.
351. *aspire*] mount up to, attain.
353. *winter's snake*] Snakes move with difficulty in winter and so may be
caught more easily; to avoid this, they may be thought to exercise utmost
caution.
354. *who*] whoever.

II.i.0.2. *Attendants*] The Quarto edition names '*little Iaques the Moore*'
among these; but he has no part in the dialogue and almost certainly
represents a character invented by Webster only to be discarded later.
3. *dove-house*] ironic; doves were proverbially innocent, loving, and tame.
5. *pole-cats*] often used abusively; they are destructive, ferret-like animals,
with a fetid smell.
haunt] have resort.
7. *cousin*] used generally of one's kin, commonly for niece or nephew.

    Marcello, see it fitted.

Marcello. My lord—the duke is here.

Francisco.   Sister, away;

    You must not yet be seen.

Isabella.   I do beseech you   10

    Entreat him mildly; let not your rough tongue

    Set us at louder variance. All my wrongs

    Are freely pardoned, and I do not doubt

    As men to try the precious unicorn's horn

    Make of the powder a preservative circle   15

    And in it put a spider, so these arms

    Shall charm his poison, force it to obeying

    And keep him chaste from an infected straying.

Francisco. I wish it may. Be gone.

                            Exit [ISABELLA].

          Enter BRACCIANO, *and* FLAMINEO.

                    Void the chamber.—

             [*Exeunt* FLAMINEO, MARCELLO,

               GIOVANNI, *and* Attendants.]

    You are welcome; will you sit? I pray, my lord,   20

    Be you my orator, my heart's too full,—

    I'll second you anon.

Monticelso.   Ere I begin

    Let me entreat your grace forgo all passion

    Which may be raisèd by my free discourse.

Bracciano. As silent as i'th'church—you may proceed.   25

Monticelso. It is a wonder to your noble friends

    That you that have as 'twere entered the world

    14–18.] Reputed specimens from the horn of the fabled unicorn commanded huge prices; it was thought that only twenty whole horns were to be found in Europe. Isabella describes a test which was to be performed by the Royal Society in London in 1661: if the spider leaves the circle, the specimen is not genuine. She also alludes to the horn's supposed power as a charm against poison.

    18. *infected*] (1) tainted (with poison); (2) depraved, immoral.

    19.S.D.] The comings and goings are awkward, perhaps intentionally so, to stress the contrived nature of the occasion.

    19. *Void*] empty, clear.

With a free sceptre in your able hand,
And have to th'use of nature well applied
High gifts of learning, should in your prime age   30
Neglect your awful throne for the soft down
Of an insatiate bed. O my lord,
The drunkard after all his lavish cups
Is dry, and then is sober; so at length,
When you awake from this lascivious dream,   35
Repentance then will follow, like the sting
Placed in the adder's tail. Wretched are princes
When fortune blasteth but a petty flower
Of their unwieldy crowns, or ravisheth
But one pearl from their sceptre; but alas!   40
When they to wilful shipwreck loose good fame,
All princely titles perish with their name.

Bracciano. You have said, my lord,—
Monticelso.   Enough to give you taste
How far I am from flattering your greatness?
Bracciano. Now you that are his second, what say you?   45
Do not like young hawks fetch a course about;
Your game flies fair and for you.
Francisco.   Do not fear it.
I'll answer you in your own hawking phrase:
Some eagles that should gaze upon the sun
Seldom soar high, but take their lustful ease,   50
Since they from dunghill birds their prey can seize.

---

28. *free*] of unrestricted power.

29. *use of nature*] i.e. profit, or advantage, of natural capacity.

31. *awful*] commanding fear and obedience.

36–7. *sting . . . tail*] adders were popularly supposed to bite with both head and tail.

38. *flower*] i.e. jewel; 'crown' (l. 39) was used of a garland of flowers.

41. *loose*] See I.i.208n.; 'shipwreck' suggests that modern 'loose' is the dominant meaning here.

42. *titles*] (1) rank; (2) rights, possessions.

name] good name, honour.

46.] 'Most commonly if a young hawk be let fly at old game, she will turn tail, and cowardly give it over' (Turberville, *Falconry*).

49.] The eagle was said to be the only bird that could gaze at the sun.

50. *ease*] Because it would make them less brave and skilful, trained hawks were not allowed to pursue easy prey.

You know Vittoria,—

Bracciano.   Yes.

Francisco.   You shift your shirt there
    When you retire from tennis.

Bracciano.   Happily.

Francisco. Her husband is lord of a poor fortune,
    Yet she wears cloth of tissue,—

Bracciano.   What of this?   55
    Will you urge that, my good lord cardinal,
    As part of her confession at next shrift,
    And know from whence it sails?

Francisco.   She is your strumpet,—

Bracciano. Uncivil sir, there's hemlock in thy breath
    And that black slander. Were she a whore of mine,   60
    All thy loud cannons and thy borrowed Switzers,
    Thy galleys, nor thy sworn confederates,
    Durst not supplant her.

Francisco.   Let's not talk on thunder.
    Thou hast a wife, our sister; would I had given
    Both her white hands to death, bound and locked fast   65
    In her last winding-sheet, when I gave thee
    But one.

Bracciano.   Thou hadst given a soul to God then.

Francisco.   True.
    Thy ghostly father, with all's absolution,
    Shall ne'er do so by thee.

Bracciano.   Spit thy poison,—

Francisco. I shall not need; lust carries her sharp whip   70

52–3. *You . . . tennis*] i.e. you use her house regularly for intimate purposes.

53. *Happily*] haply, perhaps (with pun on 'contentedly').

55. *cloth of tissue*] rich cloth, often interwoven with gold or silver.

61. *Switzers*] Swiss mercenaries were often used in feuds between Italian noblemen.

63. *supplant*] overthrow, dispossess.

64. *our*] my.

66–7. *when . . . one*] Francisco regrets that he gave the hand of his sister Isabella in marriage to Bracciano.

67. *Thou . . . God*] perhaps a sneer at Isabella's profession of piety.

68. *Thy ghostly father*] the priest who confesses you.

all's absolution] all his authority to pronounce forgiveness of sins.

At her own girdle. Look to't, for our anger
Is making thunder-bolts.
Bracciano.   Thunder? In faith,
They are but crackers.
Francisco.   We'll end this with the cannon.
Bracciano. Thou'lt get nought by it but iron in thy wounds
And gunpowder in thy nostrils.
Francisco.   Better that   75
Than change perfumes for plasters,—
Bracciano.   Pity on thee.
'Twere good you'd show your slaves or men condemned
Your new-ploughed forehead. Defiance!—and I'll meet
thee,
Even in a thicket of thy ablest men.
Monticelso. My lords, you shall not word it any further   80
Without a milder limit.
Francisco.   Willingly.
Bracciano. Have you proclaimed a triumph, that you bait
A lion thus?
Monticelso.   My lord.
Bracciano.   I am tame, I am tame, sir.
Francisco. We send unto the duke for conference
'Bout levies 'gainst the pirates; my lord duke   85
Is not at home. We come ourself in person;
Still my lord duke is busied;—but we fear
When Tiber to each prowling passenger
Discovers flocks of wild ducks, then my lord—
'Bout moulting time I mean—we shall be certain   90
To find you sure enough and speak with you.
Bracciano.   Ha?

---

73. *but*] mere.
crackers] (1) fireworks; (2) boasts.
75. *gunpowder . . . nostrils*] i.e. your cannon will not harm me, only annoy
you.
76. *change . . . plasters*] i.e. after indulgence, reap venereal disease.
78. *new-ploughed*] i.e. newly furrowed with anger.
82. *bait*] enrage, as if for a fight in a Roman spectacle or 'triumph'.
89. *wild ducks*] i.e. prostitutes.
90. *moulting time*] an allusion to loss of hair through venereal disease.

Francisco. A mere tale of a tub; my words are idle,—
But to express the sonnet by natural reason,

Enter GIOVANNI.

When stags grow melancholic you'll find the season—
Monticelso. No more, my lord. Here comes a champion   95
Shall end the difference between you both,
Your son the prince Giovanni. See, my lords,
What hopes you store in him; this is a casket
For both your crowns, and should be held like dear.
Now is he apt for knowledge; therefore know   100
It is a more direct and even way
To train to virtue those of princely blood
By examples than by precepts. If by examples,
Whom should he rather strive to imitate
Than his own father? Be his pattern, then;   105
Leave him a stock of virtue that may last,
Should fortune rend his sails and split his mast.
Bracciano. Your hand, boy. Growing to a soldier?
Giovanni. Give me a pike.
Francisco. What, practising your pike so young, fair coz?   110
Giovanni. Suppose me one of Homer's frogs, my lord,
    Tossing my bulrush thus. Pray, sir, tell me:
    Might not a child of good discretion

---

92. *tale of a tub*] cock-and-bull story; also an allusion to the sweating-tub used to cure venereal disease.

93. *express . . . reason*] put it simply, explain this cunning matter scientifically.

94. *When . . . melancholic*] A month or six weeks after rutting, a stag will go apart from the herd until its rank smell has gone.

season] appropriate time, with perhaps an allusion to the salt used in the sweating tub (see l. 92, n.).

95. *champion*] Giovanni enters wearing the armour he had been promised (see ll. 6–8 above).

99. *like dear*] equally dearly by both of you.

101. *even*] straightforward, just.

106. *stock*] (1) lineage; (2) store, fund.

110. *pike*] with sexual innuendo.

111–12. *Homer's . . . bulrush*] from *The Battle of Frogs and Mice*, a burlesque Homeric epic in which the frogs comically arm themselves with bulrushes for pikes or spears.

　　Be leader to an army?
Francisco.　　　　　　　Yes, cousin, a young prince
　　Of good discretion might.
Giovanni.　　　　　　Say you so?　　　　　115
　　Indeed I have heard 'tis fit a general
　　Should not endanger his own person oft,
　　So that he make a noise, when he's a'horseback
　　Like a Dansk drummer,—O, 'tis excellent!
　　He need not fight, methinks his horse as well　　120
　　Might lead an army for him. If I live
　　I'll charge the French foe in the very front
　　Of all my troops, the foremost man.
Francisco.　　　　　　　What, what?
Giovanni. And will not bid my soldiers up and follow
　　But bid them follow me.
Bracciano.　　　　　Forward lapwing!　　　　125
　　He flies with the shell on's head.
Francisco.　　　　　　Pretty cousin,—
Giovanni. The first year, uncle, that I go to war,
　　All prisoners that I take I will set free
　　Without their ransom.
Francisco.　　　　　Ha, without their ransom!
　　How then will you reward your soldiers　　130
　　That took those prisoners for you?
Giovanni.　　　　　　　Thus, my lord:
　　I'll marry them to all the wealthy widows
　　That fall that year.
Francisco.　　　　Why then the next year following
　　You'll have no men to go with you to war.
Giovanni. Why then I'll press the women to the war,　　135

---

115. *discretion*] Giovanni's reply suggests that his uncle is mocking him by taking his 'discretion' (l. 113) in the Falstaffian sense of 'prudence' (knowing when to hang back).

118. *So that*] so long as.

119. *Dansk*] Danish.

125. *lapwing*] a type of precocity; the bird was said to run from the nest as soon as hatched, carrying part of its shell with it.

126. *flies*] (1) leaves the nest; (2) escapes.

133. *That fall*] i.e. of the men that fall in battle.

135. *press*] impress, forcibly draft.

And then the men will follow.
Monticelso.   Witty prince.
Francisco. See a good habit makes a child a man,
          Whereas a bad one makes a man a beast.
          Come, you and I are friends.
Bracciano.   Most wishedly,
          Like bones which, broke in sunder and well set,   140
          Knit the more strongly.
Francisco. [*To Attendant off-stage*] Call Camillo hither.—
          You have received the rumour, how Count Lodowick
          Is turned a pirate.
Bracciano.   Yes.
Francisco.   We are now preparing
          Some ships to fetch him in.

                    [*Enter* ISABELLA.]

                              Behold your duchess.—
          We now will leave you and expect from you   145
          Nothing but kind entreaty.
Bracciano.   You have charmed me.
              Exeunt FRANCISCO, MONTICELSO, GIOVANNI.
          You are in health, we see.
Isabella.   And above health
          To see my lord well,—
Bracciano.   So. I wonder much
          What amorous whirlwind hurried you to Rome—
Isabella. Devotion, my lord.
Bracciano.   Devotion?   150
          Is your soul charged with any grievous sin?
Isabella. 'Tis burdened with too many, and I think
          The oft'ner that we cast our reckonings up,
          Our sleeps will be the sounder.
Bracciano.   Take your chamber.
Isabella. Nay, my dear lord, I will not have you angry,—   155
          Doth not my absence from you two months

144.S.D.] Perhaps Isabella has been listening for the right moment to
reappear.

150. *Devotion*] Isabella means love for her husband; but Bracciano wilfully
misinterprets her to mean religious devotion.

Merit one kiss?

Bracciano.   I do not use to kiss.

If that will dispossess your jealousy,

I'll swear it to you.

Isabella.   O my lovèd lord,

I do not come to chide. My jealousy?   160

I am to learn what that Italian means.

You are as welcome to these longing arms

As I to you a virgin.

Bracciano.   O, your breath!

Out upon sweet meats, and continued physic!

The plague is in them.

Isabella.   You have oft for these two lips   165

Neglected cassia or the natural sweets

Of the spring violet,—they are not yet much withered.

My lord, I should be merry,—these your frowns

Show in a helmet lovely, but on me,

In such a peaceful interview methinks   170

They are too too roughly knit.

Bracciano.   O dissemblance!

Do you bandy factions 'gainst me? Have you learnt

The trick of impudent baseness to complain

Unto your kindred?

Isabella.   Never, my dear lord.

Bracciano. Must I be haunted out, or was't your trick   —175

To meet some amorous gallant here in Rome

That must supply our discontinuance?

Isabella. I pray, sir, burst my heart, and in my death

Turn to your ancient pity, though not love.

---

157. *I . . . use*] it is not my habit, practice.

161. *am . . . learn*] am ignorant of (a common phrase).

Italian] Italians were proverbially jealous.

166. *cassia*] luxurious perfume (a poetic usage).

172. *bandy*] (1) band together; (2) threaten to raise.

174. *Never*] Lines 9–19, at the beginning of this scene, show that this is not strictly true; she had enlisted her kindred's help, saying that she forgave the 'wrongs' she had suffered and that her embraces would keep him chaste in future.

175. *haunted*] visited (its usual meaning); with wordplay on 'hunted'.

177. *supply our discontinuance*] replace me.

179. *ancient*] former, noble.

Bracciano. Because your brother is the corpulent duke,   180
　　　That is the great duke,—'Sdeath, I shall not shortly
　　　Racket away five hundred crowns at tennis
　　　But it shall rest upon record. I scorn him
　　　Like a shaved Polack; all his reverent wit
　　　Lies in his wardrobe; he's a discreet fellow   185
　　　When he's made up in his robes of state.
　　　Your brother the great duke, because h'as galleys,
　　　And now and then ransacks a Turkish fly-boat,
　　　(Now all the hellish Furies take his soul,)
　　　First made this match,—accursèd be the priest   190
　　　That sang the wedding mass, and even my issue.
Isabella. O, too too far you have cursed.
Bracciano.　　　　　　　　　　　Your hand I'll kiss,—
　　　This is the latest ceremony of my love;
　　　Henceforth I'll never lie with thee, by this,
　　　This wedding-ring; I'll ne'er more lie with thee.   195
　　　And this divorce shall be as truly kept
　　　As if the judge had doomed it. Fare you well;
　　　Our sleeps are severed.
Isabella.　　　　　　　　Forbid it the sweet union
　　　Of all things blessèd! Why, the saints in heaven
　　　Will knit their brows at that.
Bracciano.　　　　　　　　　　Let not thy love   200
　　　Make thee an unbeliever. This my vow
　　　Shall never, on my soul, be satisfied
　　　With my repentance. Let thy brother rage
　　　Beyond a horrid tempest or sea-fight;
　　　My vow is fixèd.
Isabella.　　　　　　O my winding-sheet,   205

---

182. *Racket away*] i.e. lose by wagering on a tennis match.
183. *rest upon record*] i.e. be held against me.
184. *Like . . . Polack*] i.e. as of no account; Poles were said to be careless of taking lives and to shave all their heads except a very long forelock.
188. *fly-boat*] small, fast sailing boat, or pinnace.
191. *my issue*] i.e. my son, fruit of the wedding.
193. *latest*] last.
197. *doomed it*] pronounced it as a sentence.
198. *union*] agreement, joint pronouncement.
202. *satisfied*] fulfilled, discharged.
204. *horrid*] dreadful.

Now shall I need thee shortly! Dear my lord,
Let me hear once more, what I would not hear,—
Never?
Bracciano. Never.
Isabella. O my unkind lord, may your sins find mercy,   210
  As I upon a woeful widowed bed
  Shall pray for you, if not to turn your eyes
  Upon your wretched wife and hopeful son,
  Yet that in time you'll fix them upon heaven.
Bracciano. No more.—Go, go, complain to the great duke.   215
Isabella. No, my dear lord, you shall have present witness
  How I'll work peace between you. I will make
  Myself the author of your cursèd vow;
  I have some cause to do it, you have none;
  Conceal it, I beseech you, for the weal   220
  Of both your dukedoms, that you wrought the means
  Of such a separation; let the fault
  Remain with my supposèd jealousy,—
  And think with what a piteous and rent heart
  I shall perform this sad ensuing part.   225

  Enter FRANCISCO, FLAMINEO, MONTICELSO, MARCELLO.

Bracciano. Well, take your course.—My honourable brother!
Francisco. Sister,—This is not well, my lord,—why, sister!—
  She merits not this welcome.
Bracciano.   Welcome, say?
  She hath given a sharp welcome.
Francisco.   Are you foolish?
  Come, dry your tears. Is this a modest course   230
  To better what is nought, to rail and weep?
  Grow to a reconcilement, or by heaven
  I'll ne'er more deal between you.
Isabella.   Sir, you shall not,
  No, though Vittoria upon that condition
  Would become honest.

---

  221. *both your dukedoms*] i.e. the Orsini and (by his wife) the de Medici
lineage.
  231. *nought*] (1) of little account; (2) wicked, worthless.
  235. *honest*] chaste.

Francisco.   Was your husband loud   235
    Since we departed?
Isabella.   By my life, sir, no;
    I swear by that I do not care to lose.
    Are all these ruins of my former beauty
    Laid out for a whore's triumph?
Francisco.   Do you hear?—
    Look upon other women, with what patience   240
    They suffer these slight wrongs, with what justice
    They study to requite them,—take that course.
Isabella. O that I were a man, or that I had power
    To execute my apprehended wishes,
    I would whip some with scorpions.
Francisco.   What? Turned Fury?   245
Isabella. To dig the strumpet's eyes out, let her lie
    Some twenty months a-dying, to cut off
    Her nose and lips, pull out her rotten teeth,
    Preserve her flesh like mummia, for trophies
    Of my just anger! Hell to my affliction   250
    Is mere snow-water. By your favour, sir—
    Brother draw near, and my lord cardinal—
    Sir, let me borrow of you but one kiss,
    Henceforth I'll never lie with you, by this,
    This wedding-ring.
Francisco.   How? Ne'er more lie with him?   255
Isabella. And this divorce shall be as truly kept
    As if in throngèd court a thousand ears
    Had heard it and a thousand lawyers' hands
    Sealed to the separation.
Bracciano. Ne'er lie with me?
Isabella.   Let not my former dotage   260
    Make thee an unbeliever; this my vow

---

   237. *by that . . . lose*] i.e. by my chastity.
   242. *study*] endeavour, take pains.
   244. *apprehended*] conscious, fully understood.
   245. *whip . . . scorpions*] an Old Testament phrase; 'scorpions' were
knotted or barbed whips.
   Fury] avenging goddess.
   249. *mummia*] See I.i.16n.
   261. *Make . . . unbeliever*] cause you to doubt what I am saying now.

Shall never, on my soul, be satisfied
With my repentance,—*manet alta mente repostum.*
Francisco. Now by my birth you are a foolish, mad,
And jealous woman.
Bracciano.   You see 'tis not my seeking.   265
Francisco. Was this your circle of pure unicorn's horn
You said should charm your lord? Now horns upon thee,
For jealousy deserves them. Keep your vow,
And take your chamber.
Isabella. No, sir, I'll presently to Padua;   270
I will not stay a minute.
Monticelso.   O good madam.
Bracciano. 'Twere best to let her have her humour;
Some half day's journey will bring down her stomach,
And then she'll turn in post.
Francisco.   To see her come
To my lord cardinal for a dispensation   275
Of her rash vow will beget excellent laughter.
Isabella. Unkindness, do thy office; poor heart, break!
Those are the killing griefs which dare not speak.   *Exit.*

Enter CAMILLO.

Marcello. Camillo's come, my lord.
Francisco. Where's the commission?   280
Marcello. 'Tis here.
Francisco. Give me the signet.
Flamineo. [*To Bracciano*] My lord, do you mark their whisper-
ing? I will compound a medicine out of their two heads,
stronger than garlic, deadlier than stibium; the can-   285

---

263. manet . . . repostum] It shall be treasured up in the depths of my
mind (Virgil, *Aeneid*, I.26).

267. *horns upon thee*] i.e. may your husband be unfaithful.

273. *stomach*] pride, obstinacy.

274. *turn in post*] return post-haste.

278.] a common proverb.

282. *signet*] signet ring, for sealing the commission.

283.S.D. To Bracciano] Flamineo and Bracciano walk apart, the others,
busy with the commission, retiring to the rear of the stage until l. 323.

285. *stibium*] metallic antimony (used as a poison).

285-6. *cantharides*] Spanish fly; medicinal, but poisonous if used
unadvisedly; they could be applied externally, as a counter-irritant. Their
secret working is Webster's own invention.

tharides, which are scarce seen to stick upon the flesh
when they work to the heart, shall not do it with more
silence or invisible cunning.

Enter Doctor [JULIO].

Bracciano. About the murder.

Flamineo. They are sending him to Naples, but I'll send him   290
to Candy. Here's another property too.

Bracciano. O, the doctor,—

Flamineo. A poor quack-salving knave, my lord, one that
should have been lashed for's lechery, but that he
confessed a judgement, had an execution laid upon him,   295
and so put the whip to a *non plus*.

Julio. And was cozened, my lord, by an arranter knave than
myself, and made pay all the colourable execution.

Flamineo. He will shoot pills into a man's guts, shall make
them have more ventages than a cornet or a lamprey; he   300
will poison a kiss, and was once minded, for his master-
piece, because Ireland breeds no poison, to have prepared a deadly vapour in a Spaniard's fart that should
have poisoned all Dublin.

---

291. *to Candy*] i.e. to death; the inhabitants of Candy, or Crete, were said
to live on serpents, making nourishing food of this poisonous reptile.

291. *property*] instrument.

293. *quack-salving*] working as a quack-doctor.

294–8. *should . . . execution*] i.e. when Julio was convicted of lechery, he
pretended that he had been previously convicted and sentenced for debt, and
so was taken into custody and thus escaped whipping; in the end, however,
he was cheated by another rogue who announced that he was the creditor
and so received payment according to the supposed judgement.

296. *a* non plus] a state in which no more can be done, a state of being
unprepared or perplexed.

297. *cozened*] cheated.

298. *colourable*] plausible.

300. *cornet*] simple musical instrument of the oboe class.

lamprey] a fish with prominent cavities (*ventages*) on either side for convey-
ing water to and from the gills.

301. *poison a kiss*] i.e. prepare a surface with poison so that the victim will
kiss it; see II.ii.23. S.D.

302. *Ireland . . . poison*] Serpents were said to have been banished in re-
sponse to St Patrick's prayers.

303–4. *should have*] was intended to have.

Bracciano. O Saint Anthony's fire!   305
Julio. Your secretary is merry, my lord.
Flamineo. O thou cursed antipathy to nature,—look, his eye's
    bloodshed like a needle a chirurgeon stitcheth a wound
    with,—let me embrace thee, toad, and love thee, O thou
    abhominable loathsome gargarism, that will fetch up   310
    lungs, lights, heart, and liver by scruples.
Bracciano. No more.—I must employ thee, honest doctor;
    You must to Padua, and by the way
    Use some of your skill for us.
Julio.   Sir, I shall.
Bracciano. But for Camillo?   315
Flamineo. He dies this night by such a politic strain,
    Men shall suppose him by's own engine slain.
    But for your duchess' death?
Julio.   I'll make her sure—
Bracciano. Small mischiefs are by greater made secure.
Flamineo. Remember this, you slave: when knaves come to   320
    preferment, they rise as gallowses are raised i'th'Low
    Countries, one upon another's shoulders.

                          Exeunt [BRACCIANO, FLAMINEO, *and*
                                    Doctor JULIO].
Monticelso. Here is an emblem, nephew—pray peruse it.

---

  305. *Saint . . . fire*] erysipelas, a disease causing inflammation of the skin.
  308. *bloodshed*] bloodshot.
chirurgeon] surgeon.
  310. *abhominable*] This spelling, from the original Quarto, suggests that
the common and erroneous etymology *ab homine* is implied here.
gargarism] gargle.
  311. *scruples*] very small quantities or portions.
  316. *He dies*] i.e. Flamineo takes on himself responsibility for this murder.
politic] ingenious.
strain] (1) force, compulsion; (2) spraining of muscles (in the vaulting-
horse practise Flamineo has already arranged).
  317. *engine*] contrivance.
  319.] a common proverb.
  321. *gallowses*] those condemned to the gallows.
  322. *one . . . shoulders*] Gallows were improvised on the field of battle by
having one prisoner stand on the shoulders of another who then steps aside,
leaving his fellow prisoner hanging.
  323. *emblem*] a drawing expressing a moral fable or allegory.

'Twas thrown in at your window,—
Camillo.   At my window?
Here is a stag, my lord, hath shed his horns,   325
And for the loss of them the poor beast weeps—
The word, '*Inopem me copia fecit*'.
Monticelso. That is,
Plenty of horns hath made him poor of horns.
Camillo. What should this mean?
Monticelso.   I'll tell you. 'Tis given out   330
You are a cuckold.
Camillo.   Is it given out so?
I had rather such report as that, my lord,
Should keep within doors.
Francisco.   Have you any children?
Camillo. None, my lord.
Francisco.   You are the happier—
I'll tell you a tale.
Camillo.   Pray my lord.
Francisco.   An old tale.   335
Upon a time Phoebus the god of light
(Or him we call the sun) would need be married.
The gods gave their consent, and Mercury
Was sent to voice it to the general world.
But what a piteous cry there straight arose   340
Amongst smiths, and felt-makers, brewers and cooks,
Reapers and butter-women, amongst fishmongers
And thousand other trades, which are annoyed
By his excessive heat; 'twas lamentable.
They came to Jupiter all in a sweat   345
And do forbid the banns; a great fat cook

---

327. *word*] motto.
Inopem . . . fecit] Abundance has made me destitute; from Ovid's *Meta-morphoses* where Narcissus complains to his reflection. The most obvious application would be that Camillo, being rich in the beauty of his wife, would be better off if he had no wife at all. Monticelso, however, applies it another way, playing on a double sense of 'horn': being plentifully a cuckold, Camillo has no sexual satisfaction.

333. *keep . . . doors*] Camillo puns weakly on 'given out': (1) published, reported; (2) sent forth.

334. *You . . . happier*] reversing the proverbial wisdom that children make a man blessed and happy.

Was made their speaker, who entreats of Jove
That Phoebus might be gelded, for if now
When there was but one sun, so many men
Were like to perish by his violent heat,   350
What should they do if he were married
And should beget more, and those children
Make fireworks like their father?—so say I,
Only I will apply it to your wife,—
Her issue (should not providence prevent it)   355
Would make both nature, time, and man repent it.

Monticelso. Look you, cousin,
    Go change the air, for shame; see if your absence
    Will blast your cornucopia. Marcello
    Is chosen with you joint commissioner   360
    For the relieving our Italian coast
    From pirates.

Marcello.   I am much honoured in't.

Camillo.   But, sir,
    Ere I return the stag's horns may be sprouted,
    Greater than these are shed.

Monticelso.   Do not fear it;
    I'll be your ranger.

Camillo.   You must watch i'th'nights;   365
    Then's the most danger.

Francisco.   Farewell, good Marcello.
    All the best fortunes of a soldier's wish
    Bring you a'shipboard.

Camillo. Were I not best, now I am turned soldier,
    Ere that I leave my wife, sell all she hath,   370
    And then take leave of her?

Monticelso.   I expect good from you,
    Your parting is so merry.

Camillo. Merry my lord, a'th'captain's humour right—
    I am resolvèd to be drunk this night.

                  Exit [CAMILLO *with* MARCELLO].

---

353. *fireworks*] alluding to the 'fire' of Phoebus and that of sexual ardour.
358. *Go . . . air*] Leave this place.
359. *cornucopia*] 'horn of plenty', ironically applied to the cuckold's horn.
365. *ranger*] (1) game-keeper; (2) libertine.

Francisco. So,—'twas well fitted; now shall we discern   375
    How his wished absence will give violent way
    To Duke Bracciano's lust.
Monticelso.   Why, that was it;
    To what scorned purpose else should we make choice
    Of him for a sea-captain? And besides,
    Count Lodowick, which was rumoured for a pirate,   380
    Is now in Padua.
Francisco.   Is't true?
Monticelso.   Most certain.
    I have letters from him, which are suppliant
    To work his quick repeal from banishment,—
    He means to address himself for pension
    Unto our sister duchess.
Francisco.   O, 'twas well.   385
    We shall not want his absence past six days,—
    I fain would have the Duke Bracciano run
    Into notorious scandal, for there's nought
    In such curst dotage, to repair his name,
    Only the deep sense of some deathless shame.   390
Monticelso. It may be objected I am dishonourable,
    To play thus with my kinsman, but I answer,
    For my revenge I'd stake a brother's life,
    That being wronged durst not avenge himself.
Francisco. Come to observe this strumpet.
Monticelso.   Curse of greatness!   395
    Sure he'll not leave her.
Francisco.   There's small pity in't;
    Like mistletoe on sere elms spent by weather,
    Let him cleave to her and both rot together.   *Exeunt.*

---

385. *sister*] a polite manner of speaking, not implying blood relationship.
Monticelso is uncle to Isabella's husband.

388–90. *there's . . . shame*] As Isabella's brother, Francisco is concerned
chiefly with Bracciano's name which Giovanni will inherit; only a scandal
would be able to make Bracciano change course and so save the family
honour.

395. *Curse of*] this is the curse that afflicts.

396. *pity*] cause for pity.

397. *sere*] dry, withered.

[II. ii]

Enter BRACCIANO *with one in the habit of*
a Conjurer.

Bracciano. Now, sir, I claim your promise. 'Tis dead midnight,
    The time prefixed to show me by your art
    How the intended murder of Camillo
    And our loathed duchess grow to action.
Conjurer. You have won me by your bounty to a deed   5
    I do not often practise. Some there are,
    Which by sophistic tricks aspire that name
    Which I would gladly lose, of nigromancer;
    As some that use to juggle upon cards,
    Seeming to conjure, when indeed they cheat;   10
    Others that raise up their confederate spirits
    'Bout windmills, and endanger their own necks,
    For making of a squib, and some there are
    Will keep a curtal to show juggling tricks
    And give out 'tis a spirit; besides these   15
    Such a whole ream of almanac-makers, figure-flingers—
    Fellows indeed that only live by stealth,
    Since they do merely lie about stol'n goods—

II.ii.0.1.] The location is a room in Camillo's house (see ll. 50–1 below).

8. *nigromancer*] necromancer; this form implies an association with 'black art' (Latin *niger*), instead of the correct derivation from *necro*, death, + *manteia*, divination, hence, prophesying by means of communication with the dead.

9. *use to juggle*] practise magic.

12. *windmills*] fanciful schemes or projects.

13. *squib*] firework, usually small and insignificant.

14–15. *keep . . . spirit*] an allusion to 'Mr Banks', a travelling showman of the 1590s, who exhibited a performing horse; after 1595, it was a docked bay gelding (or 'curtal') called Morocco. Its 'tricks' included dancing, feigning death, counting money and reacting suitably to the names of Queen Elizabeth or the King of Spain. Some reported that the horse eventually ate its master, others that both were burned at Rome for witchcraft; in fact, Mr Banks retired to become a vintner in Cheapside, London.

16. *ream*] (1) ream of paper; (2) realm.

figure-flingers] makers of horoscopes (contemptuous).

17–18. *only . . . goods*] i.e. live only by secret cunning and by taking what is not theirs, that is, by lying about spirits and powers which are not theirs by right.

They'd make men think the devil were fast and loose,
With speaking fustian Latin. Pray sit down,   20
Put on this night-cap sir, 'tis charmed,—and now
I'll show you by my strong-commanding art
The circumstance that breaks your duchess' heart.

A dumb show.

Enter suspiciously, JULIO *and another; they draw a curtain where*
BRACCIANO's *picture is; they put on spectacles of glass, which cover their
eyes and noses, and then burn perfumes afore the picture, and wash the
lips of the picture; that done, quenching the fire, and putting off their
spectacles, they depart laughing.*

Enter ISABELLA *in her nightgown as to bed-ward, with lights after her,
Count* LODOVICO, GIOVANNI, *and others waiting on her; she kneels
down as to prayers, then draws the curtain of the picture, does three
reverences to it, and kisses it thrice; she faints and will not suffer them to
come near it, dies; sorrow expressed in* GIOVANNI *and in* Count
LODOVICO; *she's conveyed out solemnly.*

Bracciano. Excellent, then she's dead,—
Conjurer.   She's poisoned,
By the fumed picture. 'Twas her custom nightly,   25
Before she went to bed, to go and visit

19–20. *They'd . . . Latin*] By speaking incomprehensibly these quacks
would make people believe they had conjured up the devil and he was on the
rampage.

fast and loose] (1) shifty, inconstant (originally = a cheating game); (2) free
to do anything.

fustian] inflated, bombastic.

Latin] the language used to exorcise or conjure up devils.

23.1. dumb show] This theatrical device was originally an allegorical or
simplified presentation of events which were to follow in a fully dramatized
form (see 'The Mouse-trap' in *Hamlet*), but it came to be used as a means of
compressing the action of a drama.

23.2. another] The Quarto names 'Christophero', but Webster has given
no individuality to this character.

curtain] commonly used to protect paintings.

23.4. wash] i.e. anoint with a liquid poison.

23.8. others] While keeping this general direction, the Quarto also names
'Guid-antonio' after Giovanni; again no distinction is given to the character,
suggesting that Webster had dispensed with it while writing the scene.

Your picture, and to feed her eyes and lips
On the dead shadow; Doctor Julio,
Observing this, infects it with an oil
And other poisoned stuff, which presently　　　　　30
Did suffocate her spirits.

Bracciano.　　　　　　　　　Methought I saw
　Count Lodowick there.

Conjurer.　　　　　　　　　He was, and by my art
　I find he did most passionately dote
　Upon your duchess. Now turn another way,
　And view Camillo's far more politic fate.—　　　　　35
　Strike louder music from this charmèd ground,
　To yield, as fits the act, a tragic sound!

The second dumb show.

Enter FLAMINEO, MARCELLO, CAMILLO, *with four more as Captains;
they drink healths and dance; a vaulting-horse is brought into the room;*
MARCELLO *and two more whispered out of the room while* FLAMINEO
and CAMILLO *strip themselves into their shirts, as to vault; compliment
who shall begin; as* CAMILLO *is about to vault,* FLAMINEO *pitcheth him
upon his neck, and with the help of the rest writhes his neck about, seems
to see if it be broke, and lays him folded double as 'twere under the horse,
makes shows to call for help;* MARCELLO *comes in, laments, sends for the*
Cardinal [MONTICELSO] *and* Duke [FRANCISCO], *who comes forth
with armed men; wonder at the act;* [FRANCISCO] *commands the body to
be carried home, apprehends* FLAMINEO, MARCELLO, *and the rest, and
[all] go as 'twere to apprehend* VITTORIA.

Bracciano. 'Twas quaintly done, but yet each circumstance
　I taste not fully.

Conjurer.　　　　　O, 'twas most apparent.
　You saw them enter charged with their deep healths　　　　　40
　To their boon voyage, and, to second that,

---

30. *presently*] immediately.

35. *politic*] cunningly contrived.

37.4.] whispered . . . room] are made to leave the room on some whispered pretext.

38. *quaintly*] skilfully.

40. *charged . . . healths*] given a farewell with drinking of toasts.

41. *boon*] prosperous.

Flamineo calls to have a vaulting-horse
Maintain their sport. The virtuous Marcello
Is innocently plotted forth the room,
Whilst your eye saw the rest, and can inform you   45
The engine of all.

Bracciano. It seems Marcello and Flamineo
Are both committed.

Conjurer.   Yes, you saw them guarded,
And now they are come with purpose to apprehend
Your mistress, fair Vittoria; we are now   50
Beneath her roof. 'Twere fit we instantly
Make out by some back postern.

Bracciano.   Noble friend,
You bind me ever to you; this shall stand
As the firm seal annexèd to my hand.
It shall enforce a payment.

Conjurer.   Sir, I thank you.   55

                         Exit BRACCIANO.

Both flowers and weeds spring when the sun is warm,
And great men do great good, or else great harm.

                         Exit Conjurer.

[III. i]

> *Enter* FRANCISCO, *and* MONTICELSO, *their* Chancellor
> *and* Register.

Francisco. You have dealt discreetly to obtain the presence
Of all the grave lieger ambassadors
To hear Vittoria's trial.

Monticelso.   'Twas not ill,

---

44. *plotted . . . room*] made to leave the room as was designed in the plot.
46. *engine*] means, contrivance.
49. *they*] i.e. Monticelso and Francisco's armed attendants.
52. *postern*] secret gate.
53. *this*] i.e. this service you have done, or, in view of 'bind', this hand-shake (with a quibble on 'hand' of l. 54).
54. *annexèd . . . hand*] affixed to my signature.
56.] proverbial.

III.i.0.1.] This scene is located in an antechamber to the papal consistory or courtroom.
2. *lieger*] resident (in Rome).

For, sir, you know we have nought but circumstances
To charge her with, about her husband's death;   5
Their approbation therefore to the proofs
Of her black lust shall make her infamous
To all our neighbouring kingdoms. I wonder
If Bracciano will be here.
Francisco.   O fie,
'Twere impudence too palpable.   [*Exeunt.*]   10

Enter FLAMINEO *and* MARCELLO *guarded, and*
a Lawyer.

Lawyer. What, are you in by the week? So—I will try now
  whether thy wit be close prisoner. Methinks none should
  sit upon thy sister but old whoremasters,—
Flamineo. Or cuckolds, for your cuckold is your most terrible
  tickler of lechery; whoremasters would serve, for none are   15
  judges at tilting but those that have been old tilters.
Lawyer. My lord duke and she have been very private.
Flamineo. You are a dull ass; 'tis threatened they have been
  very public.
Lawyer. If it can be proved they have but kissed one another—   20
Flamineo. What then?
Lawyer. My lord cardinal will ferret them,—
Flamineo. A cardinal I hope will not catch conies.
Lawyer. For to sow kisses (mark what I say), to sow kisses is

---

10.S.D. Exeunt] Ferdinand and Monticelso leave together, probably still
talking; the officials will leave in their own time, overlapping with the following entry.

10.2. *Lawyer*] In contrast to the one in III.ii, this lawyer knows so little of
law and affects to know so much about the court, that he may be a different
character; perhaps the stage direction should read 'Courtier'.

11. *are . . . week*] have they caught you.

13. *sit upon*] sit in judgement upon.

15. *tickler*] (1) chastiser; (2) exciter.

16. *tilting*] (1) jousting; (2) copulating.

17. *private*] intimate.

19. *public*] (1) unconcealed; (2) licentious (a 'public woman' was a prostitute). Flamineo's joke is that their 'private' behaviour has been 'public' and
notorious.

22. *ferret*] question searchingly, go for. (See next note.)

23. *catch conies*] a common cant phrase meaning 'to cheat fools'; used here
because (1) 'ferret', another cant phrase, implied using ferrets to catch
'conies' or rabbits , and (2) 'cony' was also used for 'woman', with either
endearment or indecency.

to reap lechery, and I am sure a woman that will endure   25
kissing is half won.

Flamineo. True, her upper part by that rule; if you will win her
nether part too, you know what follows.

Lawyer. Hark the ambassadors are lighted,—

Flamineo. [*Aside*] I do put on this feignèd garb of mirth   30
To gull suspicion.

Marcello. O my unfortunate sister!
I would my dagger's point had cleft her heart
When she first saw Bracciano. You, 'tis said,
Were made his engine and his stalking horse   35
To undo my sister.

Flamineo.   I made a kind of path
To her and mine own preferment.

Marcello.   Your ruin.

Flamineo. Hum! Thou art a soldier,
Followest the great duke, feedest his victories,
As witches do their serviceable spirits,   40
Even with thy prodigal blood,—what hast got?
But like the wealth of captains, a poor handful,
Which in thy palm thou bear'st, as men hold water—
Seeking to gripe it fast, the frail reward
Steals through thy fingers.

Marcello.   Sir,—

Flamineo.   Thou hast scarce maintenance   45
To keep thee in fresh chamois.

Marcello.   Brother!

Flamineo.   Hear me,—
And thus when we have even poured ourselves
Into great fights, for their ambition
Or idle spleen, how shall we find reward?

---

29. *lighted*] alighted from horseback or carriage.

31. *gull*] deceive.

35. *engine*] instrument, tool, pandar.

40. *serviceable*] diligent in service. Witches were thought to breastfeed or
otherwise give their bodies to the spirits that did their bidding.

42. *the wealth of captains*] Military men proverbially ended up with no
wealth to show for their pains.

43. *palm*] ironic allusion to 'bearing the palm' (i.e. gaining victory); also
the palm of the hand.

46. *chamois*] chamois jerkins, worn under armour.

But as we seldom find the mistletoe   50
Sacred to physic on the builder oak
Without a mandrake by it, so in our quest of gain.
Alas, the poorest of their forced dislikes
At a limb proffers, but at heart it strikes.
This is lamented doctrine.
Marcello.   Come, come.   55
Flamineo. When age shall turn thee
White as a blooming hawthorn,—
Marcello.   I'll interrupt you.
For love of virtue bear an honest heart,
And stride over every politic respect,
Which where they most advance they most infect.   60
Were I your father, as I am your brother,
I should not be ambitious to leave you
A better patrimony.

Enter Savoy [Ambassador].

Flamineo.   I'll think on't.—
The lord ambassadors.

Here there is a passage of the lieger Ambassadors *over
the stage severally.*
Enter French Ambassador.

Lawyer. O, my sprightly Frenchman, do you know him? He's   65
  an admirable tilter.
Flamineo. I saw him at last tilting; he showed like a pewter
  candlestick fashioned like a man in armour, holding a
  tilting-staff in his hand, little bigger than a candle of
  twelve i'th' pound.   70

50–2.] i.e. as poison (such as the root of the *mandrake*) is usually found
close to what is good (or medicinal) and secure, so success and ruin go
together.

51. *builder*] used for building.

53–4.] i.e. When great men take offence at the most trivial action, they
appear to give light punishment, but in fact the loss of their favour destroys
all the offender's hopes of future success.

59. *politic respect*] consideration having to do with advancement at court.

64.1–2. passage . . . severally] i.e. as if on their way to Vittoria's
arraignment.

67–70.] probably with sexual innuendo (a candle weighing a twelfth of a
pound is very small); see next note and note at l. 16 above.

Lawyer. O, but he's an excellent horseman.
Flamineo. A lame one in his lofty tricks; he sleeps a'horseback
   like a poulter,—

         Enter English *and* Spanish [Ambassadors.]

Lawyer. Lo you, my Spaniard.
Flamineo. He carries his face in's ruff, as I have seen a serving-   75
   man carry glasses in a cypress hat-band, monstrous
   steady for fear of breaking; he looks like the claw of a
   blackbird, first salted and then broiled in a candle.

                                             Exeunt.

[III. ii]

         THE ARRAIGNMENT OF VITTORIA.

   Enter FRANCISCO, MONTICELSO, *the six lieger* Ambassadors,
   BRACCIANO, VITTORIA, [ZANCHE, FLAMINEO, MARCELLO],
                 Lawyer, *and a* Guard.

Monticleso. [*To Bracciano*] Forbear, my lord, here is no place
      assigned you;
      This business by his holiness is left
      To our examination.
Bracciano.   May it thrive with you.
                       Lays a rich gown under him.
Francisco. A chair there for his lordship.
Bracciano. Forbear your kindness. An unbidden guest   5

72–3.] 'lofty tricks' (used of acrobatics and tumbling), 'sleeps', 'horseback', and the common association of horse/whores, indicate a run of sexual
innuendo.
   poulter] poulterer, with a possible pun on 'palterer' (see V.iii.57n.).
   75. *carries . . . ruff*] Spanish pomposity and love of wide ruffs were common subjects for mockery.
   76. *cypress*] fine lawn or crepe.
   78. *broiled in*] grilled over.

III.ii.0.1.] The location is a consistory (or ecclesiastical courtroom) in
Rome. A scene-title is unusual in playtexts at this time; it suggests that time
is taken (perhaps during the previous scene) to furnish the stage appropri-
ately and that everyone (except Bracciano) enters formally to take up their
assigned places.

> Should travail as Dutch women go to church:
> Bear their stools with them.
>
> *Monticelso.*   At your pleasure, sir.
> Stand to the table, gentlewoman. Now, signior,
> Fall to your plea.
>
> *Lawyer.* *Domine judex converte oculos in hanc pestem mulierum*   10
> *corruptissimam.*
>
> *Vittoria.* What's he?
>
> *Francisco.*   A lawyer, that pleads against you.
>
> *Vittoria.* Pray, my lord, let him speak his usual tongue—
> I'll make no answer else.
>
> *Francisco.*   Why, you understand Latin.
>
> *Vittoria.* I do, sir, but amongst this auditory   15
> Which come to hear my cause, the half or more
> May be ignorant in't.
>
> *Monticelso.*   Go on, sir:—
>
> *Vittoria.*   By your favour,
> I will not have my accusation clouded
> In a strange tongue; all this assembly
> Shall hear what you can charge me with.
>
> *Francisco.*   Signior,   20
> You need not stand on't much; pray change your
>   language.
>
> *Monticelso.* O, for God sake; gentlewoman, your credit
> Shall be more famous by it.
>
> *Lawyer.*   Well then have at you.
>
> *Vittoria.* I am at the mark, sir, I'll give aim to you,
> And tell you how near you shoot.   25
>
> *Lawyer.* Most literated judges, please your lordships
> So to connive your judgements to the view

---

6. *travail*] (1) journey; (2) work laboriously.

10–11.] My lord judge, turn your eyes upon this plague, the most corrupted of women.

21. *stand*] insist.

22. *credit*] reputation.

23. *famous*] infamous.

have at you] here goes, *en gard*.

24. *give aim*] act as a marker at the butts.

26. *literated*] learned (a new and italianate word).

27. *connive*] The lawyer is too pompous for his own good, in effect saying
the opposite of what he wishes to convey; to 'connive' should mean to
'overlook'.

>Of this debauched and diversivolent woman,
>Who such a black concatenation
>Of mischief hath effected, that to extrip   30
>The memory of 't must be the consummation
>Of her and her projections—

Vittoria.   What's all this—?

Lawyer. Hold your peace.
>Exorbitant sins must have exulceration.

Vittoria. Surely, my lords, this lawyer here hath swallowed   35
>Some pothecary's bills or proclamations,
>And now the hard and undigestible words
>Come up like stones we use give hawks for physic.
>Why, this is Welsh to Latin.

Lawyer.   My lords, the woman
>Knows not her tropes nor figures, nor is perfect   40
>In the academic derivation
>Of grammatical elocution.

Francisco.   Sir, your pains
>Shall be well spared, and your deep eloquence
>Be worthily applauded amongst those
>Which understand you.

Lawyer.   My good lord!

Francisco.   Sir,   45
>Put up your papers in your fustian bag,—

>   FRANCISCO *speaks this as in scorn.*

>Cry mercy, sir, 'tis buckram,—and accept
>My notion of your learned verbosity.

Lawyer. I most graduatically thank your lordship.

---

28. *diversivolent*] desiring strife (the word was evidently made up for the occasion).

32. *projections*] projects (more legal double-talk).

34. *must have exulceration*] must be probed and excised like an ulcer.

38.] an actual cure recommended to falconers.

39. *to*] compared with (Welsh is, to the English, gibberish, even worse than Latin).

42. *elocution*] expression.

46. *fustian*] (1) coarse cloth; (2) inflated, bombastic.

47. *buckram*] coarse linen, with a suggestion of stiffness and a false appearance of strength.

49. *graduatically*] in the manner of a graduate (probably another word made up for the occasion).

I shall have use for them elsewhere.   [*Exit.*]   50
Monticelso. I shall be plainer with you, and paint out
   Your follies in more natural red and white
   Than that upon your cheek.
Vittoria.   O, you mistake.
   You raise a blood as noble in this cheek
   As ever was your mother's.   55
Monticelso. I must spare you till proof cry whore to that.—
   Observe this creature here, my honoured lords,
   A woman of a most prodigious spirit
   In her effected.
Vittoria.   Honourable my lord,
   It doth not suit a reverend cardinal   60
   To play the lawyer thus.
Monticelso. O, your trade instructs your language!
   You see, my lords, what goodly fruit she seems,
   Yet, like those apples travellers report
   To grow where Sodom and Gomorrah stood,   65
   I will but touch her and you straight shall see
   She'll fall to soot and ashes.
Vittoria.   Your envenomed
   Pothecary should do't.
Monticelso.   I am resolved
   Were there a second paradise to lose
   This devil would betray it.
Vittoria.   O poor charity!   70
   Thou art seldom found in scarlet.
Monticelso. Who knows not how, when several night by night
   Her gates were choked with coaches, and her rooms

51–3. *be plainer . . . cheek*] i.e. forgo the 'colours' of rhetoric and portray you (Vittoria) as you really are.
  paint out] depict.
  59. *effected*] possibly 'put into effect, fulfilled'; but the sense is forced; perhaps the text should read 'affected', meaning 'cherished, desired'.
  64–7.] The legend derives from Deuteronomy, xxxii.32, where the grapes growing in Sodom and Gomorrah are said to be bitter to the taste.
  67–8. *Your . . . do't*] i.e. If I should thus fall, it would be because you had hired a druggist to poison me.
  68. *resolved*] convinced.
  71. *scarlet*] the colour of a cardinal's vestments and a judge's robes. Seldom can true charity be found in a cardinal, says Vittoria.

ed the stars with several kind of lights,
e did counterfeit a prince's court   75
, banquets and most riotous surfeits?
    This whore, forsooth, was holy.
Vittoria.   Ha? Whore—what's that?
Monticelso. Shall I expound whore to your? sure I shall;
    I'll give their perfect character. They are, first,
    Sweet-meats which rot the eater; in man's nostril   80
    Poisoned perfumes. They are coz'ning alchemy,
    Shipwrecks in calmest weather. What are whores?
    Cold Russian winters, that appear so barren
    As if that nature had forgot the spring.
    They are the true material fire of hell,   85
    Worse than those tributes i'th'Low Countries paid,
    Exactions upon meat, drink, garments, sleep—
    Ay, even on man's perdition, his sin.
    They are those brittle evidences of law
    Which forfeit all a wretched man's estate   90
    For leaving out one syllable. What are whores?
    They are those flattering bells have all one tune,
    At weddings and at funerals; your rich whores
    Are only treasuries by extortion filled,
    And emptied by cursed riot. They are worse,   95
    Worse than dead bodies, which are begged at gallows
    And wrought upon by surgeons, to teach man
    Wherein he is imperfect. What's a whore?
    She's like the guilty counterfeited coin
    Which whosoe'er first stamps it brings in trouble   100
    All that receive it.
Vittoria.   This character 'scapes me.

---

79. *character*] sketch of a character-type (like those in *New Characters*, 1615, to which Webster almost certainly contributed).

86. *tributes*] local taxes on travellers were reported to equal or exceed the value of goods or services received.

88. *perdition*] i.e. prostitution.

89–91. *brittle . . . syllable*] scribal omission of a single word could invalidate legal title.

97. *surgeons*] The Company of Barber Surgeons in London was allowed the bodies of four executed felons each year for use in anatomy classes.

99. *guilty*] with wordplay on the 'gilt' used by a coiner.

101. *'scapes me*] (1) escapes me, is unintelligible; (2) goes right past me, doesn't touch me.

Monticelso. You gentlewoman?
    Take from all beasts and from all minerals
    Their deadly poison—
Vittoria.   Well what then?
Monticelso.   I'll tell thee—
    I'll find in thee a pothecary's shop   105
    To sample them all.
French Ambassador.   She hath livèd ill.
English Ambassador. True, but the cardinal's too bitter.
Monticelso. You know what whore is—next the devil,
    Adult'ry,
    Enters the devil, Murder.
Francisco.   Your unhappy
    Husband is dead.
Vittoria.   O he's a happy husband   110
    Now he owes nature nothing.
Francisco. And by a vaulting engine.
Monticelso.   An active plot—
    He jumped into his grave.
Francisco.   What a prodigy was't,
    That from some two yards' height a slender man
    Should break his neck?
Monticelso.   I' th' rushes.
Francisco.   And what's more,   115
    Upon the instant lose all use of speech,
    All vital motion, like a man had lain
    Wound up three days. Now mark each circumstance.
Monticelso. And look upon this creature was his wife.
    She comes not like a widow; she comes armed   120
    With scorn and impudence. Is this a mourning habit?
Vittoria. Had I foreknown his death as you suggest,
    I would have bespoke my mourning.
Monticelso. O, you are cunning.
Vittoria. You shame your wit and judgement   125
    To call it so; what, is my just defence

---

108. *next*] after.
111.] now that he has paid back his debt to nature by giving up his life.
112. *vaulting engine*] vaulting horse.
   plot] with pun on 'engine' = 'device'.
115. *rushes*] used as floor-covering; also an emblem of fragility.
118. *Wound up*] i.e. in his winding sheet.
123. *bespoke my mourning*] ordered mourning attire for myself.

By him that is my judge called impudence?
Let me appeal then from this Christian court
To the uncivil Tartar.
Monticelso.   See, my lords,
She scandals our proceedings.
Vittoria.   Humbly thus,   130
Thus low, to the most worthy and respected
Lieger ambassadors, my modesty
And womanhood I tender; but withal
So entangled in a cursèd accusation
That my defence, of force like Perseus,   135
Must personate masculine virtue. To the point:
Find me but guilty, sever head from body,
We'll part good friends; I scorn to hold my life
At yours or any man's entreaty, sir.
English Ambassador. She hath a brave spirit.   140
Monticelso. Well, well, such counterfeit jewels
Make true ones oft suspected.
Vittoria.   You are deceived;
For know that all your strict-combinèd heads,
Which strike against this mine of diamonds,
Shall prove but glassen hammers; they shall break,—   145
These are but feignèd shadows of my evils.
Terrify babes, my lord, with painted devils;
I am past such needless palsy. For your names
Of whore and murd'ress, they proceed from you,
As if a man should spit against the wind,   150

---

128. *Christian*] (1) ecclesiastical (the 'Courts Christian' were the English
Ecclesiastical Courts dealing with adultery); (2) civilized.

129. *uncivil*] barbarous, with a pun on the 'Civil Courts'.

130. *scandals*] abuses, disgraces.

135. *of force*] necessarily.

Perseus] son of Danae and Zeus who, with the help of Athena, killed
Medusa, the Gorgon who turned all those who looked at her to stone; in
Jonson's *Masque of Queens* (1609), Perseus represents 'heroic and masculine
virtue'.

143. *strict-combinèd*] closely or secretly allied.

heads] (1) the judges' heads; (2) military and political forces; (3) hammer-
heads.

146. *shadows*] often used of portraits as contrasted with their originals.

148. *palsy*] shaking.

For] as for.

The filth returns in's face.

Monticelso. Pray you, mistress, satisfy me one question:
   Who lodged beneath your roof that fatal night
   Your husband brake his neck?

Bracciano.   That question
   Enforceth me break silence. I was there.   155

Monticelso. Your business?

Bracciano.   Why, I came to comfort her,
   And take some course for settling her estate,
   Because I heard her husband was in debt
   To you, my lord.

Monticelso.   He was.

Bracciano.   And 'twas strangely feared
   That you would cozen her.

Monticelso.   Who made you overseer?   160

Bracciano. Why my charity, my charity, which should flow
   From every generous and noble spirit
   To orphans and to widows.

Monticelso.   Your lust.

Bracciano. Cowardly dogs bark loudest. Sirrah priest,
   I'll talk with you hereafter.—Do you hear?   165
   The sword you frame of such an excellent temper,
   I'll sheathe in your own bowels;
   There are a number of thy coat resemble
   Your common post-boys.

Monticelso.   Ha?

Bracciano.   Your mercenary post boys,—
   Your letters carry truth, but 'tis your guise   170
   To fill your mouths with gross and impudent lies.

Servant. My lord, your gown.

Bracciano.   Thou liest—'twas my stool.

---

159. *strangely*] uncommonly, extremely.

164. *Cowardly . . . loudest*] a common proverb.

Sirrah] insultingly used (usually reserved for inferiors).

166. *sword*] instrument of justice.

168. *thy*] a change to the insulting second person singular.

coat] profession.

170. *guise*] custom, practice.

172.] In his anger, Bracciano has forgotten the cloak he was sitting on; by calling his cloak a 'stool' he implies that he has not been treated with the respect due to his rank and honour.

Bestow't upon thy master that will challenge
The rest a'th'household stuff—for Bracciano
Was ne'er so beggarly to take a stool   175
Out of another's lodging; let him make
Valance for his bed on't, or a demi-foot-cloth
For his most reverend moil.—Monticelso,
Nemo me impune lacessit.   *Exit* BRACCIANO.
Monticelso. Your champion's gone.
Vittoria.   The wolf may prey the better.   180
Francisco. My lord, there's great suspicion of the murder,
     But no sound proof who did it. For my part
     I do not think she hath a soul so black
     To act a deed so bloody; if she have,
     As in cold countries husbandmen plant vines,   185
     And with warm blood manure them, even so
     One summer she will bear unsavoury fruit,
     And ere next spring wither both branch and root.
     The act of blood let pass, only descend
     To matter of incontinence.
Vittoria.   I discern poison   190
     Under your gilded pills.
Monticelso. Now the duke's gone, I will produce a letter,
     Wherein 'twas plotted he and you should meet,
     At an apothecary's summer-house,
     Down by the river Tiber—view't, my lords—   195
     Where after wanton bathing and the heat
     Of a lascivious banquet . . . I pray read it,
     I shame to speak the rest.
Vittoria.   Grant I was tempted;
     Temptation to lust proves not the act.

173-4. *Bestow't . . . stuff*] Bracciano mockingly implies that Monticelso
controls, personally, the entire court proceedings.
   173. *challenge*] lay claim to.
   177. *Valance*] bed-curtain.
   on't] of it.
   demi-foot-cloth] half-length covering for a horse (see I.ii.51n.).
   178. *moil*] mule, with wordplay on 'moil' = drudgery.
   179.] No one injures me with impunity.
   190. *incontinence*] unchastity.
   194. *summer-house*] arbour, garden-house.

Casta est quam nemo rogavit;   200
You read his hot love to me, but you want
My frosty answer.

Monticelso.   Frost i'th'dog-days! Strange!

Vittoria. Condemn you me for that the duke did love me?
So may you blame some fair and crystal river
For that some melancholic distracted man   205
Hath drowned himself in't.

Monticelso.   Truly, drowned indeed.

Vittoria. Sum up my faults, I pray, and you shall find
That beauty and gay clothes, a merry heart,
And a good stomach to a feast, are all,
All the poor crimes that you can charge me with.   210
In faith, my lord, you might go pistol flies;
The sport would be more noble.

Monticelso.   Very good.

Vittoria. But take you your course; it seems you have
beggared me first
And now would fain undo me. I have houses,
Jewels, and a poor remnant of crusadoes;   215
Would those would make you charitable.

Monticelso.   If the devil
Did ever take good shape, behold his picture.

Vittoria. You have one virtue left:
You will not flatter me.

Francisco.   Who brought this letter?

Vittoria. I am not compelled to tell you.   220

Monticelso. My lord duke sent to you a thousand ducats,
The twelfth of August.

Vittoria.   'Twas to keep your cousin

200.] She is chaste whom no man has solicited (Ovid, *Amores*).

201. *want*] lack.

202. *dog-days*] days when the sun is near the Dog-star, the hottest and most unwholesome time of year; the forty days following 11 August.

206. *drowned*] Monticelso plays on the sense 'drowned in sin'.

211. *pistol*] shoot with a pistol.

215. *crusadoes*] Portuguese coins of gold or silver.

216–17. *devil . . . shape*] a direct reference to the play's title; see 2 Corinthians, xi.14: 'Satan himself is transformed into an angel of light'.

222. *cousin*] i.e. nephew (Camillo). See II.i.323.

From prison; I paid use for't.
Monticelso.   I rather think
   'Twas interest for his lust.
Vittoria. Who says so but yourself? If you be my accuser,   225
   Pray cease to be my judge; come from the bench;
   Give in your evidence 'gainst me, and let these
   Be moderators. My lord cardinal,
   Were your intelligencing ears as long
   As to my thoughts, had you an honest tongue,   230
   I would not care though you proclaimed them all.
Monticelso. Go to, go to.
   After your goodly and vainglorious banquet,
   I'll give you a choke-pear.
Vittoria.   A' your own grafting?
Monticelso. You were born in Venice, honourably descended   235
   From the Vitelli; 'twas my cousin's fate—
   Ill may I name the hour—to marry you;
   He bought you of your father.
Vittoria.   Ha?
Monticelso. He spent there in six months
   Twelve thousand ducats, and to my acquaintance   240
   Received in dowry with you not one julio;
   'Twas a hard penny-worth, the ware being so light.
   I yet but draw the curtain; now to your picture.
   You came from thence a most notorious strumpet,
   And so you have continued.
Vittoria.   My lord—
Monticelso.   Nay hear me,   245
   You shall have time to prate. My Lord Bracciano—

---

223. *use*] interest, usury.
224. *his*] Bracciano's.
229. *intelligencing*] spying, acting as informer.
230. *As to*] i.e. as to reach to.
234. *choke-pear*] hard, unpalatable pear (often used figuratively for a severe rebuke or setback).
235–6. *born . . . Vitelli*] In fact, Vittoria was born at Gubbio and descended from the Accoramboni; Venice was known for luxury and vice, while the Vitelli were a high-profile Roman family.
241. *julio*] a papal coin of small value.
242. *light*] a common quibble: (1) of little weight; (2) unchaste.
243.] See II.ii.23.2n.

Alas, I make but repetition
Of what is ordinary and Rialto talk,
And ballated, and would be played a'th'stage,
But that vice many times finds such loud friends   250
That preachers are charmed silent.—
You gentlemen, Flamineo and Marcello,
The court hath nothing now to charge you with,
Only you must remain upon your sureties
For your appearance.

Francisco.   I stand for Marcello.   255

Flamineo. And my lord duke for me.

Monticelso. For you, Vittoria, your public fault,
Joined to th'condition of the present time,
Takes from you all the fruits of noble pity.
Such a corrupted trial have you made   260
Both of your life and beauty, and been styled
No less in ominous fate than blazing stars
To princes; here's your sentence: you are confined
Unto a house of convertites, and your bawd—

Flamineo. [*Aside*] Who, I?

Monticelso.   The Moor.

Flamineo.   [*Aside*] O, I am a sound man again.   265

Vittoria. A house of convertites, what's that?

Monticelso.   A house
Of penitent whores.

Vittoria.   Do the noblemen in Rome
Erect it for their wives, that I am sent
To lodge there?

Francisco. You must have patience.

Vittoria.   I must first have vengeance.   270
I fain would know if you have your salvation
By patent, that you proceed thus.

Monticelso.   Away with her.

---

248. *Rialto talk*] talk of the town, gossip.
249. *ballated*] Ballad-makers were the popular journalists of the time.
251. *charmed*] i.e. bought off.
254. *sureties*] bail.
255. *stand for*] guarantee the appearance in court of.
257. *public*] See III.i.19 and n.
272. *patent*] special licence.

Take her hence.
Vittoria. A rape, a rape.
Monticelso.   How?
Vittoria.   Yes, you have ravished justice,
Forced her to do your pleasure.
Monticelso.   Fie, she's mad—   275
Vittoria. Die with those pills in your most cursèd maw.
Should bring you health, or, while you sit a'th'bench,
Let your own spittle choke you.
Monticelso.   She's turned Fury.
Vittoria. That the last day of judgement may so find you,
And leave you the same devil you were before.   280
Instruct me some good horse-leech to speak treason,
For, since you cannot take my life for deeds,
Take it for words.—O woman's poor revenge
Which dwells but in the tongue! I will not weep,
No I do scorn to call up one poor tear   285
To fawn on your injustice. Bear me hence,
Unto this house of—what's your mitigating title?
Monticelso. Of convertites.
Vittoria. It shall not be a house of convertites;
My mind shall make it honester to me   290
Than the Pope's palace, and more peaceable
Than thy soul, though thou art a cardinal.
Know this, and let it somewhat raise your spite:
Through darkness diamonds spread their richest light.
             Exit VITTORIA [*with* ZANCHE, *guarded*].

             Enter BRACCIANO.

Bracciano. Now you and I are friends, sir, we'll shake hands, 295
In a friend's grave, together, a fit place,
Being the emblem of soft peace t'atone our hatred.
Francisco. Sir, what's the matter?
Bracciano. I will not chase more blood from that loved cheek;

276–7. *Die . . . health*] i.e. May you die of a dose of your own medicine.
281–3. *Instruct . . . words*] i.e. Torture me so that I incriminate myself, and then, since you have no proof of guilty actions on my part, execute me on the basis of a forced confession.
281. *horse-leech*] i.e. blood-sucker.
297. *atone*] appease.

You have lost too much already. Fare you well. [*Exit.*] 300
Francisco. How strange these words sound! What's the
   interpretation?
Flamineo. [*Aside*] Good, this is a preface to the discovery of
   the duchess' death. He carries it well. Because now I
   cannot counterfeit a whining passion for the death of my 305
   lady, I will feign a mad humour for the disgrace of my
   sister, and that will keep off idle questions. Treason's
   tongue hath a villainous palsy in't; I will talk to any man,
   hear no man, and for a time appear a politic madman.
                                                       [*Exit.*]

        Enter GIOVANNI, Count LODOVICO.

Francisco. How now, my noble cousin, what, in black?   310
Giovanni. Yes uncle, I was taught to imitate you
   In virtue, and you must imitate me
   In colours for your garments. My sweet mother
   Is—
Francisco. How? Where?   315
Giovanni. Is there,—no, yonder,—indeed, sir, I'll not tell
      you,
   For I shall make you weep.
Francisco. Is dead.
Giovanni. Do not blame me now,
   I did not tell you so.
Lodovico.   She's dead, my lord.   320
Francisco. Dead?
Monticelso. Blessed lady; thou art now above thy woes.—
   Will't please your lordships to withdraw a little?
                                 [*Exeunt* Ambassadors.]
Giovanni. What do the dead do, uncle? Do they eat,
   Hear music, go a-hunting, and be merry,   325
   As we that live?

307–8. *Treason's . . . in't*] i.e. a traitor cannot help saying more than he
should.
   palsy] uncontrolled nervousness.
   309. *politic madman*] i.e. using craft to feign a politically convenient
madness.
   310. *cousin*] nephew.

Francisco. No, coz; they sleep.

Giovanni.   Lord, Lord, that I were dead!
    I have not slept these six nights. When do they wake?

Francisco. When God shall please.

Giovanni.   Good God, let her sleep ever.
    For I have known her wake an hundred nights,   330
    When all the pillow, where she laid her head,
    Was brine-wet with her tears.
    I am to complain to you, sir.
    I'll tell you how they have used her, now she's dead:
    They wrapped her in a cruel fold of lead,   335
    And would not let me kiss her.

Francisco.   Thou didst love her.

Giovanni. I have often heard her say she gave me suck,
    And it should seem by that she dearly loved me,
    Since princes seldom do it.

Francisco. O, all of my poor sister that remains!   340
    Take him away, for God's sake.

                    [*Exit* GIOVANNI *attended.*]

Monticelso.   How now, my lord?

Francisco. Believe me, I am nothing but her grave,
    And I shall keep her blessèd memory
    Longer than thousand epitaphs.   [*Exeunt.*]

[III. iii]

        Enter FLAMINEO *as distracted*[, MARCELLO,
                and LODOVICO].

Flamineo. We endure the strokes like anvils or hard steel,
    Till pain itself make us no pain to feel.
    Who shall do me right now? Is this the end of service?
    I'd rather go weed garlic; travail through France, and be
    mine own ostler; wear sheep-skin linings; or shoes that   5

---

333. *I am to*] I must.
335. *fold*] wrapping; or clasp, embrace (in association with 'cruel' and
'kiss', ll. 335–6).

III.iii.0.1.] The location is back in the antechamber of III.i.
4. *travail*] work (my) way.
5. *linings*] underwear.

stink of blacking; be entered into the list of the forty
thousand pedlars in Poland.

Enter Savoy [Ambassador].

Would I had rotted in some surgeon's house at Venice,
built upon the pox as well as on piles, ere I had served
Bracciano.   10
Savoy Ambassador. You must have comfort.
Flamineo. Your comfortable words are like honey. They relish
well in your mouth that's whole; but in mine that's
wounded they go down as if the sting of the bee were in
them. O, they have wrought their purpose cunningly, as if   15
they would not seem to do it of malice. In this a politician
imitates the devil, as the devil imitates a cannon.
Wheresoever he comes to do mischief, he comes with his
backside towards you.

Enter the French [Ambassador].

French Ambassador. The proofs are evident.   20
Flamineo. Proof! 'Twas corruption. O gold, what a god art
thou! And O man, what a devil art thou to be tempted by
that cursed mineral! Yon diversivolent lawyer; mark him,
knaves turn informers, as maggots turn to flies,—you
may catch gudgeons with either. A cardinal—I would he   25
would hear me—there's nothing so holy but money will
corrupt and putrify it, like victual under the line.

Enter English Ambassador.

You are happy in England, my lord; here they sell justice

---

7. *Poland*] noted at this time for poverty and huge distances.

9. *pox*] venereal disease (the curing of which has made the 'surgeon' or
doctor wealthy).

piles] (1) wooden foundations driven into water; (2) haemorrhoids.

18–19. *Wheresoever . . . you*] Witches were believed to kiss the devil's but-
tocks in token of obedience.

23. *diversivolent*] mocking the lawyer's language; see III.ii.28 and n.

25. *gudgeons*] small fish, easily caught and used as bait; often used of
gullible simpletons.

27. *under the line*] i.e. at the equator, where food 'corrupts' or rots
quickly.

with those weights they press men to death with. O
horrible salary!   30

English Ambassador. Fie, fie, Flamineo.

Flamineo. Bells ne'er ring well till they are at their full pitch,
and I hope yon cardinal shall never have the grace to pray
well till he come to the scaffold.

                         [*Exeunt* Ambassadors.]

If they were racked now to know the confederacy! But   35
your noblemen are privileged from the rack; and well
may. For a little thing would pull some of them a'pieces
afore they came to their arraignment. Religion; O, how it
is commeddled with policy. The first bloodshed in the
world happened about religion. Would I were a Jew.   40

Marcello. O, there are too many.

Flamineo. You are deceived. There are not Jews enough,
priests enough, nor gentlemen enough.

Marcello. How?

Flamineo. I'll prove it. For if there were Jews enough, so many 45
Christians would not turn usurers; if priests enough, one
should not have six benefices; and if gentlement enough,

---

29. *weights . . . with*] a torture inflicted by English law until 1772 on those
refusing to plead either guilty or not guilty when charged with felonies other
than treason; if the victim died under this pressing, his family benefited in
that his goods were not confiscated because he had not been convicted.
Flamineo's meaning is intentionally obscure, but he seems to imply that in
Italy corruption prevents true justice and the victim's family can never
benefit.

30. *salary*] reward.

32. *at . . . pitch*] i.e. pulled up, inverted at their full height.

35. *racked*] tortured on the rack.

know] make known.

36–7. *well may*] i.e. with good reason.

37. *pull . . . pieces*] destroy some of them in argument; Flamineo also implies that some are so weakened by venereal disease that they are easily pulled
apart on the 'rack'.

39. *commeddled*] mixed together.

39–40. *The first . . . world*] i.e. Cain's murder of his brother Abel, in a
quarrel about how best to worship God.

46. *usurers*] 'Jew' had become almost synonymous with 'usurer'; Jews were
allowed to practise usury and then were condemned for it.

46–7. *if . . . benefices*] The passage satirizes the widespread abuse whereby
clergymen enjoyed the salaries of several church offices at once.

so many early mushrooms, whose best growth sprang
from a dunghill, should not aspire to gentility. Farewell.
Let others live by begging. Be thou one of them; practise   50
the art of Wolner in England to swallow all's given thee;
and yet let one purgation make thee as hungry again as
fellows that work in a saw-pit. I'll go hear the screech-
owl.   *Exit.*

Lodovico. [*Aside*] This was Bracciano's pandar, and 'tis
    strange   55
That in such open and apparent guilt
Of his adulterous sister he dare utter
So scandalous a passion. I must wind him.

                Enter FLAMINEO.

Flamineo. [*Aside*] How dares this banished count return to
    Rome,
His pardon not yet purchased? I have heard   60
The deceased duchess gave him pension,
And that he came along from Padua
I'th'train of the young prince. There's somewhat in't.
Physicians, that cure poisons, still do work
With counterpoisons.

Marcello.   Mark this strange encounter.   65

Flamineo. The god of melancholy turn thy gall to poison,
And let the stigmatic wrinkles in thy face,
Like to the boisterous waves in a rough tide,
One still overtake another!

Lodovico.   I do thank thee
And I do wish ingeniously for thy sake   70

---

48. *mushrooms*] upstarts; growing well on dunghills, mushrooms imply low
social origins.

51. *Wolner*] a 'singing-man of Windsor' who was famous in Webster's time
for being able to eat iron, glass, raw fish and flesh; he died after eating a raw
eel.

58. *wind him*] draw him out, discover what he intends to do.

60. *purchased*] obtained (not necessarily by payment).

67. *stigmatic*] branding with infamy, ignominious.

70. *ingeniously*] The sense is ambiguous, because this word was often used
= 'ingenuously'.

The dog-days all year long.

Flamineo.　　　　　　　　　　How croaks the raven?
Is our good duchess dead?

Lodovico.　　　　　　　　Dead—

Flamineo.　　　　　　　　　　　O fate!
Misfortune comes like the coroner's business,
Huddle upon huddle.

Lodovico. Shalt thou and I join housekeeping?

Flamineo.　　　　　　　　　　　　Yes, content.　　75
Let's be unsociably sociable.

Lodovico. Sit some three days together, and discourse.

Flamineo. Only with making faces;
Lie in our clothes.

Lodovico. With faggots for our pillows.

Flamineo.　　　　　　　　　And be lousy.　　80

Lodovico. In taffeta linings; that's gentle melancholy,—
Sleep all day.

Flamineo.　　　　　Yes; and like your melancholic hare
Feed after midnight.

Enter ANTONELLI [*and* GASPARO, *laughing*].

We are observed; see how yon couple grieve.

Lodovico. What a strange creature is a laughing fool,　　85
As if man were created to no use
But only to show his teeth.

Flamineo.　　　　　　　　I'll tell thee what,—
It would do well instead of looking-glasses
To set one's face each morning by a saucer
Of a witch's congealed blood.

Lodovico.　　　　　　　　Precious girn, rogue.　　90

---

71. *dog-days*] See III.ii.202n.
raven] proverbially ill-boding.
74. *Huddle upon huddle*] in heaps.
80. *faggots*] boundles of sticks.
lousy] infested with lice.
81. *taffeta linings*] plain-woven, glossy silk undergarments.
gentle] (1) genteel; (2) soft, comfortable.
84. *grieve*] said ironically.
89. *saucer*] receptacle used to receive the blood in blood-letting.
90. *girn*] referring to a face 'set' in a mirror of blood (see ll. 89–90): (1) snarl, grin, act of showing teeth (see l. 87); (2) snare, trap, wile.

  We'll never part.
Flamineo. Never; till the beggary of courtiers,
  The discontent of churchmen, want of soldiers,
  And all the creatures that hang manacled,
  Worse than strappadoed, on the lowest felly   95
  Of Fortune's wheel be taught in our two lives
  To scorn that world which life of means deprives.
Antonelli. My lord, I bring good news. The Pope on's death-
  bed,
  At th'earnest suit of the great Duke of Florence,
  Hath signed your pardon, and restored unto you— 100
Lodovico. I thank you for your news. Look up again,
  Flamineo, see my pardon.
Flamineo.   Why do you laugh?
  There was no such condition in our covenant.
Lodovico. Why?
Flamineo. You shall not seem a happier man than I.— 105
  You know our vow sir; if you will be merry,
  Do it i'th'like posture, as if some great man
  Sate while his enemy were executed;
  Though it be very lechery unto thee,
  Do't with a crabbèd politician's face.   110
Lodovico. Your sister is a damnable whore.
Flamineo.   Ha?
Lodovico. Look you; I spake that laughing.
Flamineo. Dost ever think to speak again?
Lodovico.   Do you hear?
  Wilt sell me forty ounces of her blood,
  To water a mandrake?
Flamineo.   Poor lord, you did vow 115

---

 95. *strappado'd*] tied with one's hands behind one's back and then hoisted
up by a rope tied to the hands.

 felly] felloe, section of the circular rim of a wheel.

 96. *Fortune's wheel*] an emblem of mutability; a personified Fortune was
fabled to turn a wheel, so raising men from its lowest 'felly' to its highest, and
then down again. Here Flamineo associates it with the 'wheel', an instrument
of torture (as in V.vi.295).

 97. *life of means deprives*] deprives life of the means of livelihood.

 109.] though it be as pleasurable to you as sex.

 115. *mandrake*] The root was said to feed on blood, and was therefore
often found near gallows; see also III.i.50–2n.

To live a lousy creature.

Lodovico.   Yes;—

Flamineo.   Like one
   That had for ever forfeited the daylight,
   By being in debt,—

Lodovico.   Ha, ha!

Flamineo. I do not greatly wonder you do break;
   Your lordship learnt long since. But I'll tell you,—   120

Lodovico. What?

Flamineo.   And't shall stick by you.

Lodovico.   I long for it.

Flamineo. This laughter scurvily becomes your face;
   If you will not be melancholy, be angry.   *Strikes him.*
   See, now I laugh too.

Marcello. You are to blame; I'll force you hence.

Lodovico.   Unhand me.   125

                    Exit MARCELLO *and* FLAMINEO.
   That e'er I should be forced to right myself
   Upon a pandar.

Antonelli.   My lord—

Lodovico. H'had been as good met with his fist a thunderbolt.

Gasparo. How this shows!

Lodovico.   Ud's death, how did my sword miss him?
   These rogues that are most weary of their lives   130
   Still scape the greatest dangers.
   A pox upon him! All his reputation—
   Nay all the goodness of his family—
   Is not worth half this earthquake.
   I learnt it of no fencer to shake thus;   135
   Come I'll forget him, and go drink some wine.   *Exeunt.*

[IV. i]

                    Enter FRANCISCO *and* MONTICELSO.

Monticelso. Come, come my lord, untie your folded
      thoughts,

---

117. *for . . . daylight*] i.e. been imprisoned for life.
119. *break*] i.e. break your oath, with a pun on 'go bankrupt'.
121. *And't . . . you*] and you'll not forget it.
129. *Ud's*] i.e. God's.

IV.i.o.1.] The location is a private room in Francisco's palace.

And let them dangle loose as a bride's hair.
Your sister's poisoned.
Francisco.   Far be it from my thoughts
   To seek revenge.
Monticelso.   What, are you turned all marble?
Francisco. Shall I defy him, and impose a war   5
   Most burdensome on my poor subjects' necks,
   Which at my will I have not power to end?
   You know, for all the murders, rapes, and thefts
   Committed in the horrid lust of war,
   He that unjustly caused it first proceed   10
   Shall find it in his grave and in his seed.
Monticelso. That's not the course I'd wish you. Pray, observe
     me;
   We see that undermining more prevails
   Than doth the cannon. Bear your wrongs concealed,
   And, patient as the tortoise, let this camel   15
   Stalk o'er your back unbruised; sleep with the lion,
   And let this brood of secure foolish mice
   Play with your nostrils, till the time be ripe
   For th'bloody audit, and the fatal gripe;
   Aim like a cunning fowler, close one eye,   20
   That you the better may your game espy.
Francisco. Free me my innocence, from treacherous acts!
   I know there's thunder yonder; and I'll stand,
   Like a safe valley, which low bends the knee
   To some aspiring mountain, since I know   25
   Treason, like spiders weaving nets for flies,
   By her foul work is found, and in it dies.
   To pass away these thoughts, my honoured lord,
   It is reported you possess a book
   Wherein you have quoted, by intelligence,   30
   The names of all notorious offenders
   Lurking about the city,—
Monticelso.   Sir, I do;

2.] In Jacobean days, virgin brides wore their hair so.
13. *undermining*] digging mines under fortifications in a siege.
16. *with the lion*] like the lion.
23. *yonder*] in heaven.
27. *found*] discovered.
30. *intelligence*] secret intelligence.

And some there are which call it my black book.
Well may the title hold; for though it teach not
The art of conjuring, yet in it lurk   35
The names of many devils.
Francisco.   Pray let's see it.
Monticelso. I'll fetch it to your lordship.

                                      Exit MONTICELSO.
Francisco.   Monticelso,
I will not trust thee, but in all my plots
I'll rest as jealous as a town besieged.
Thou canst not reach what I intend to act;   40
Your flax soon kindles, soon is out again,
But gold slow heats, and long will hot remain.

    [*Re*]*enter* MONTICELSO; *presents* FRANCISCO *with a book.*

Monticelso. 'Tis here, my lord.
Francisco. First your intelligencers—pray let's see.
Monticelso. Their number rises strangely,   45
    And some of them
    You'd take for honest men.
    Next are pandars.
    These are your pirates; and these following leaves,
    For base rogues that undo young gentlemen   50
    By taking up commodities;
    For politic bankrupts;
    For fellows that are bawds to their own wives,

---

33. *black book*] originally used of official records, later for lists of rogues
and villains; Monticelso uses it so that he puns on the 'black' art of necro-
mancy or 'conjuring' (l. 35).

39. *jealous*] suspicious, watchful.

40. *reach*] (1) understand; (2) attain.

45–8.] The line arrangement is from the Quarto; a similar arrangement is
not found elsewhere and so this may well reproduce the way Webster wrote
the lines in the manuscript and so represented Monticelso's pauses as he
points out details written in his black book.

51. *taking up commodities*] Swindlers lent goods instead of money, placing
an exaggerated value on them; they then required repayment in cash at their
valuation.

52. *politic bankrupts*] those who hid their assets, declared bankruptcy, and
then absconded leaving debts unpaid.

Only to put off horses and slight jewels,
Clocks, defaced plate, and such commodities,   55
  At birth of their first children.
Francisco.   Are there such?
Monticelso. These are for impudent bawds,
  That go in men's apparel; for usurers
  That share with scriveners for their good reportage;
  For lawyers that will antedate their writs;   60
  And some divines you might find folded there,
  But that I slip them o'er for conscience' sake.
  Here is a general catalogue of knaves.
  A man might study all the prisons o'er,
  Yet never attain this knowledge.
Francisco.   Murderers.   65
  Fold down the leaf, I pray,—
  Good my lord, let me borrow this strange doctrine.
Monticelso. Pray use't, my lord.
Francisco.   I do assure your lordship
  You are a worthy member of the state,
  And have done infinite good in your discovery   70
  Of these offenders.
Monticelso.   Somewhat, sir.
Francisco.   O God!
  Better than tribute of wolves paid in England;
  'Twill hang their skins o'th'hedge.
Monticelso.   I must make bold

54–6. *put . . . children*] i.e. force their wives' lovers to buy 'commodities' at inflated prices in return for silence and complaisance when the bastards were born.

59. *share . . . reportage*] i.e. give a percentage cut to scriveners for recommending them to clients.

60. *antedate*] i.e. fake evidence by predating documents.

61. *folded*] between the folds of the pages; also, alluding to their role as shepherds of Christ's flock, using sheepfolds.

62. *slip them o'er*] pass by them.

67. *doctrine*] (1) instruction; (2) theology.

72.] King Edgar (944–75) was said to have ordered the Welsh to pay three hundred wolves a year in tribute, in order to free the land of the ravenous animals.

73. *hang . . . hedge*] Dogs that attacked sheep were killed and so treated.

To leave your lordship.
Francisco.   Dearly sir, I thank you,—
If any ask for me at court, report   75
You have left me in the company of knaves.
                              Exit MONTICELSO.
I gather now by this, some cunning fellow
That's my lord's officer, one that lately skipped
From a clerk's desk up to a justice' chair,
Hath made this knavish summons; and intends,   80
As th'Irish rebels wont were to sell heads,
So to make prize of these. And thus it happens,
Your poor rogues pay for't, which have not the means
To present bribe in fist; the rest o'th'band
Are razed out of the knaves' record; or else   85
My lord he winks at them with easy will,
His man grows rich, the knaves are the knaves still.
But to the use I'll make of it: it shall serve
To point me out a list of murderers,
Agents for any villainy. Did I want   90
Ten leash of courtesans, it would furnish me;
Nay, laundress three armies. That in so little paper
Should lie th'undoing of so many men!
'Tis not so big as twenty declarations.
See the corrupted use some make of books: 95
Divinity, wrested by some factious blood,
Draws swords, swells battles, and o'erthrows all good.
To fashion my revenge more seriously,
Let me remember my dead sister's face;
Call for her picture; no, I'll close mine eyes,   100
And in a melancholic thought I'll frame

81.] The English army offered money for the heads of Irish rebels.

89. *point me out*] identify for me.

91. *leash*] sets of three (originally a sporting term, as of hounds, hawks, etc.).

92. *laundress*] provide with laundresses (a trade proverbially of easy virtue).

94. *declarations*] official proclamations.

96. *Divinity*] theology, religious writings.

wrested . . . blood] twisted to suit the purpose of some bloody faction.

101–3. *melancholic . . . works*] In melancholy men, 'phantasy, or imagination . . . is most powerful and strong, and often hurts, producing many

Her figure 'fore me.

Enter ISABELLA's Ghost.

               Now I ha't—how strong
Imagination works! How she can frame
Things which are not! Methinks she stands afore me;
And by the quick idea of my mind,   105
Were my skill pregnant, I could draw her picture.
Thought, as a subtle juggler, makes us deem
Things supernatural, which have cause
Common as sickness. 'Tis my melancholy.—
How cam'st thou by thy death?—How idle am I   110
To question mine own idleness?—Did ever
Man dream awake till now?—Remove this object;
Out of my brain with't! What have I to do
With tombs, or death-beds, funerals, or tears,
That have to meditate upon revenge?   115
                              [*Exit* Ghost.]
So now 'tis ended, like an old wives' story.
Statesmen think often they see stranger sights
Than madmen. Come, to this weighty business.
My tragedy must have some idle mirth in't,
Else it will never pass. I am in love,   120
In love with Corombona; and my suit
Thus halts to her in verse.—   *He writes.*
I have done it rarely. O, the fate of princes!
I am so used to frequent flattery
That being alone I now flatter myself;   125
But it will serve, 'tis sealed.

---

monstrous and prodigious things, especially if it be stirred up by some
terrible object, presented to it from common sense or memory' (Burton,
Anatomy of Melancholy).
    103. *she*] imagination.
frame] give shape to.
    105. *quick*] (1) lively, living; (2) rapid.
idea] mental picture.
    106. *pregnant*] apt and ready.
    107. *juggler*] magician.
    111. *idleness*] light-headedness, folly.
    115. *That*] I who.

Enter Servant.

Bear this
To th'house of convertites, and watch your leisure
To give it to the hands of Corombona,
Or to the matron, when some followers
Of Bracciano may be by. Away.—   130

Exit Servant.

He that deals all by strength, his wit is shallow;
When a man's head goes through, each limb will follow.
The engine for my business, bold Count Lodowick:—
'Tis gold must such an instrument procure,
With empty fist no man doth falcons lure.   135
Bracciano, I am now fit for thy encounter.
Like the wild Irish I'll ne'er think thee dead
Till I can play at football with thy head.
Flectere si nequeo superos, Acheronta movebo.   *Exit.*

[IV. ii]

Enter the Matron, *and* FLAMINEO.

Matron. Should it be known the duke hath such recourse
       To your imprisoned sister, I were like
       T'incur much damage by it.
Flamineo.   Not a scruple.
       The Pope lies on his death-bed, and their heads

---

127. *watch your leisure*] look out for a suitable moment.

132.] a proverb; usually said of a 'fox' (i.e. politician).

135.] commonly applied to human behaviour; falcons were recalled by use of a lure, a bunch of feathers etc. resembling their prey.

137–8.] The Irish were regarded by the English as savages who might desecrate a human head in this fashion.

139.] If I cannot prevail upon the gods above, I will move the infernal regions (Virgil, *Aeneid*, VII.312); Acheron is the river in Hades especially associated with pain; its name came to be used for the lower world itself, or for the Christian hell.

IV.ii.0.1.] This scene is located at first at the entrance to the house of convertites in Rome; later, at l. 71, it moves inside the house itself (see ll. 128.1).

2. *were like*] would be likely.

3. *scruple*] very small quantity.

4. *Pope*] Gregory XIII died 10 April 1585; Webster's source for the papal election (IV.iii) stresses the civil disorder which followed such events; see also ll. 211–14, below.

Are troubled now with other business   5
Than guarding of a lady.

Enter Servant.

Servant. [*Aside*] Yonder's Flamineo in conference
    With the matrona. [*To the Matron*] Let me speak with
      you.
    I would entreat you to deliver for me
    This letter to the fair Vittoria.   10
Matron. I shall, sir.

Enter BRACCIANO.

Servant.   With all care and secrecy,—
    Hereafter you shall know me, and receive
    Thanks for this courtesy.   [*Exit.*]
Flamineo.   How now? What's that?
Matron. A letter.
Flamineo.   To my sister; I'll see't delivered.
                        [*Exit* Matron.]
Bracciano. What's that you read, Flamineo?
Flamineo.   Look.   15
Bracciano. Ha? [*Reads*] '*To the most unfortunate his best re-*
    spected Vittoria'—
    Who was the messenger?
Flamineo.   I know not.
Bracciano. No! Who sent it?
Flamineo.   Ud's foot, you speak as if a man
    Should know what fowl is coffined in a baked meat   20
    Afore you cut it up.
Bracciano. I'll open't, were't her heart. What's here sub-
    scribed—
    '*Florence*'? This juggling is gross and palpable.
    I have found out the conveyance; read it, read it.
Flamineo. [*Reads*] '*Your tears I'll turn to triumphs, be but mine.*   25
    Your prop is fall'n; I pity that a vine

---

19. *Ud's foot*] by God's foot.

20. *coffined*] contained within the crust or pastry of a pie (commonly
called the 'coffin' at this time).

24. *conveyance*] (1) device, contrivance; (2) means of communicating.

26. Your prop] i.e. Bracciano; Vittoria, as a woman, is compared to a vine
growing on the strong support of a man.

Which princes heretofore have longed to gather,
Wanting supporters, now should fade and wither.'
Wine i'faith, my lord, with lees would serve his turn.
'Your sad imprisonment I'll soon uncharm,   30
And with a princely uncontrollèd arm
Lead you to Florence, where my love and care
Shall hang your wishes in my silver hair.'
A halter on his strange equivocation!
'Nor for my years return me the sad willow,—   35
Who prefer blossoms before fruit that's mellow?'
Rotten on my knowledge with lying too long
    i'th'bed-straw.
'And all the lines of age this line convinces:
The gods never wax old, no more do princes.'
A pox on't—tear it, let's have no more atheists, for God's   40
sake.

Bracciano. Ud's death, I'll cut her into atomies
    And let th'irregular north-wind sweep her up
    And blow her int' his nostrils. Where's this whore?
Flamineo. That—? What do you call her?
Bracciano.   O, I could be mad;   45
    Prevent the curst disease she'll bring me to,
    And tear my hair off. Where's this changeable stuff?

---

29. *lees*] dregs.

33.] i.e. I will take care of you in my old age.

34. *A halter*] i.e. a curse upon; literally a noose, so playing on 'hang' of
l. 33.

35.] i.e. Do not deny me just because I am old.
willow] emblem of unrequited love.

37. *bed-straw*] fruit was ripened in straw; and mattresses were commonly
filled with it. Flamineo suggests sarcastically that this writer is old and rotten
through inactivity or sexual indulgence.

38.] i.e. the following maxim (1) confutes all old maxims to the contrary;
(2) is of more force than the wrinkles associated with old age.

40. *atheists*] used, in a general sense, for impious or wicked people; but
Flamineo also means that Francisco has hubristically equated princes with
gods.

42. *Ud's death*] by God's (Christ's) death.
atomies] motes (as small as dust).

43. *irregular*] wild, unconfined.

46. *Prevent*] forestall.
disease] venereal disease (causing loss of hair).

47. *changeable stuff*] watered or shot silk; i.e. fickle woman.

Flamineo. O'er head and ears in water, I assure you,—
　　She is not for your wearing.
Bracciano.　　　　　　　　　　　In, you pandar!
Flamineo. What me, my lord? Am I your dog?　　　　　　50
Bracciano. A blood-hound. Do you brave? Do you stand me?
Flamineo. Stand you? Let those that have diseases run;
　　I need no plasters.
Bracciano. Would you be kicked?
Flamineo.　　　　　　　Would you have your neck broke?
　　I tell you, duke, I am not in Russia;　　　　　　55
　　My shins must be kept whole.
Bracciano.　　　　　　　Do you know me?
Flamineo. O my lord! methodically.
　　As in this world there are degrees of evils,
　　So in this world there are degrees of devils.
　　You're a great duke; I your poor secretary.　　　　　　60
　　I do look now for a Spanish fig, or an Italian sallet daily.
Bracciano. Pandar, ply your convoy, and leave your prating.
Flamineo. All your kindness to me is like that miserable cour-
　　tesy of Polyphemus to Ulysses,—you reserve me to be
　　devoured last,—you would dig turves out of my grave to　　65
　　feed your larks; that would be music to you. Come, I'll
　　lead you to her.

---

48. *O'er . . . water*] i.e. in deep water, with a pun on 'watered' silk (see
'wearing', l. 49).

49. *In*] Get away.

51. *brave*] defy me with bravado.
stand] confront, withstand.

52. *run*] a quibble on the 'running' sore.

55. *Russia*] Thomas Dekker's *Seven Deadly Sins* (1606) reported that
Russians beat debtors on the shins when they had money but would not pay
their debts.

57. *methodically*] through and through.

61. *look . . . sallet*] i.e. expect to be poisoned in my food.
Spanish fig] the phrase was used, with an indecent gesture of fingers and
thumb, as an expression of contempt.
sallet] salad.

62.] i.e. Shut up and attend to your trade as pandar.

64. *Polyphemus*] a Cyclops, one of a race of savage one-eyed giants, whose
hospitality consisted in eating his guests; see Homer, *Odyssey*, IX.369–70.

66. *feed*] i.e. when kept in cages; see *The Duchess of Malfi*, IV.ii.128–31.

Bracciano. Do you face me?

Flamineo. O, sir, I would not go before a politic enemy with
     my back towards him, though there were behind me a   70
     whirlpool.

          Enter VITTORIA *to* BRACCIANO *and* FLAMINEO.

Bracciano. Can you read, mistress? Look upon that letter;
     There are no characters nor hieroglyphics.
     You need no comment, I am grown your receiver,—
     God's precious, you shall be a brave great lady,   75
     A stately and advancèd whore.

Vittoria.   Say, sir?

Bracciano. Come, come, let's see your cabinet, discover
     Your treasury of love-letters. Death and furies,
     I'll see them all.

Vittoria.   Sir, upon my soul,
     I have not any. Whence was this directed?   80

Bracciano. Confusion on your politic ignorance!
                              [*Gives her the letter.*]
     You are reclaimed, are you? I'll give you the bells
     And let you fly to the devil.

Flamineo.   Ware hawk, my lord.

Vittoria. 'Florence'! This is some treacherous plot, my lord,—
     To me, he ne'er was lovely, I protest,   85
     So much as in my sleep.

Braccciano.   Right; they are plots.
     Your beauty! O, ten thousand curses on't.

---

68. *face*] (1) bully, defy; (2) face towards.

73. *characters*] emblematic, or magical, signs or writings.

74. *receiver*] i.e. pimp, receiving your love-letters.

75. *God's precious*] i.e. God's blood.
brave] grand, splendid.

76. *Say*] Do you say so?

77. *cabinet*] casket.

82. *reclaimed*] saved from wrongdoing, with wordplay on calling back a
hawk which has been let fly, or on taming a hawk.

82–3. *give . . . devil*] no longer try to keep you, but let you go to the devil;
bells were tied to a hawk's legs to aid recovery.

83. *Ware hawk*] beware a swindler, cheat (slang).

85–6. *To . . . sleep*] I never found him (Francisco) attractive, not even in
my dreams.

How long have I beheld the devil in crystal?
Thou hast led me, like an heathen sacrifice,
With music, and with fatal yokes of flowers   90
To my eternal ruin. Woman to man
Is either a god or a wolf.
Vittoria.   My lord—
Bracciano.   Away!
We'll be as differing as two adamants;
The one shall shun the other. What? Dost weep?
Procure but ten of thy dissembling trade,   95
Ye'd furnish all the Irish funerals
With howling past wild Irish.
Flamineo.   Fie, my lord.
Bracciano. That hand, that cursèd hand, which I have wearied
With doting kisses! O my sweetest duchess,
How lovely art thou now! [*To Vittoria*] Thy loose
    thoughts   100
Scatter like quicksilver; I was bewitched;
For all the world speaks ill of thee.
Vittoria.   No matter.
I'll live so now I'll make that world recant
And change her speeches. You did name your duchess.
Bracciano. Whose death God pardon.
Vittoria.   Whose death God revenge   105
On thee, most godless duke.
Flamineo.   Now for two whirlwinds.
Vittoria. What have I gained by thee but infamy?
Thou hast stained the spotless honour of my house,
And frighted thence noble society,
Like those which, sick o'th'palsy, and retain   110
Ill-scenting foxes 'bout them, are still shunned

---

88. *beheld . . . crystal*] been deceived; witches were said to see devils en-
closed and revealed in a crystal. On the other hand, small shrines were made
of crystals, with a figure of a saint inside; an allusion to the play's title is
probable.

89. *heathen sacrifice*] animal being led to a ritual slaughter.

93. *adamants*] magnets; see I.ii.172n.

96–7.] To 'weep Irish' was to wail long and loud; for funerals of wealthy
people professional mourners were hired to add to the keening.

111. *foxes*] Contact with live foxes was thought to be a cure for paralysis or
palsy.

By those of choicer nostrils.
What do you call this house?
Is this your palace? Did not the judge style it
A house of penitent whores? Who sent me to it?　　　　115
Who hath the honour to advance Vittoria
To this incontinent college? Is't not you?
Is't not your high preferment? Go, go brag
How many ladies you have undone, like me.
Fare you well, sir; let me hear no more of you.　　　　120
I had a limb corrupted to an ulcer,
But I have cut it off; and now I'll go
Weeping to heaven on crutches. For your gifts,
I will return them all; and I do wish
That I could make you full executor　　　　125
To all my sins.—O that I could toss myself
Into a grave as quickly! For all thou art worth
I'll not shed one tear more;—I'll burst first.

She throws herself upon a bed.

Bracciano. I have drunk Lethe. Vittoria?
My dearest happiness? Vittoria?　　　　130
What do you ail, my love? Why do you weep?
Vittoria. Yes, I now weep poniards, do you see?
Bracciano. Are not those matchless eyes mine?
Vittoria.　　　　　　　　　　　　　　I had rather
They were not matches.
Bracciano.　　　　　　　Is not this lip mine?
Vittoria. Yes: thus to bite it off, rather than give it thee.　　　　135
Flamineo. Turn to my lord, good sister.
Vittoria.　　　　　　　　　　　　Hence, you pandar.
Flamineo. Pandar! Am I the author of your sin?
Vittoria. Yes; he's a base thief that a thief lets in.

---

116. *advance*] possibly remembering Bracciano's first taunt, l. 76 above.

121–3. *I . . . crutches*] a reminiscence of Mark, ix.45: 'And if thy foot offend thee, cut it off; it is better for thee to enter halt into life, than having two feet to be cast into hell.'

129. *Lethe*] fabled river of forgetfulness in Hades.

132. *poniards*] daggers.

134. *not matches*] i.e. asquint; with wordplay on 'matchless', 'matches'.

138. *that . . . let in*] that lets in a thief.

Flamineo. We're blown up, my lord,—
Bracciano.   Wilt thou hear me?
    Once to be jealous of thee is t'express   140
    That I will love thee everlastingly,
    And never more be jealous.
Vittoria.   O thou fool,
    Whose greatness hath by much o'ergrown thy wit!
    What dar'st thou do, that I not dare to suffer,
    Excepting to be still thy whore? For that,   145
    In the sea's bottom sooner thou shalt make
    A bonfire.
Flamineo.   O, no oaths, for God's sake.
Bracciano. Will you hear me?
Vittoria.   Never.
Flamineo. What a damned imposthume is a woman's will!
    Can nothing break it? Fie, fie, my lord.   150
    [*Aside to Bracciano*] Women are caught as you take
        tortoises;
    She must be turned on her back. [*Aloud*] Sister, by this
        hand,
    I am on your side.—Come, come, you have wronged her.
    What a strange credulous man were you, my lord,
    To think the Duke of Florence would love her?   155
    [*Aside*] Will any mercer take another's ware
    When once 'tis toused and sullied? [*Aloud*] And yet,
        sister,
    How scurvily this frowardness becomes you!
    [*Aside*] Young leverets stand not long; and women's
        anger
    Should, like their flight, procure a little sport;   160
    A full cry for a quarter of an hour,
    And then be put to th'dead quat.

---

139. *blown up*] as by an underground mine; see *The Duchess of Malfi*,
III.ii.155–6.
    149. *imposthume*] abscess, festered swelling.
    157. *toused*] tousled, handled roughly.
    159. *leverets*] young hares.
    stand] hold out (hunting term).
    162. *quat*] squat (hunting term). The image is of a small quarried prey,
huddled over in fright.

Bracciano.   Shall these eyes,
  Which have so long time dwelt upon your face,
  Be now put out?
Flamineo. No cruel landlady i'th'world, which lends forth
  groats to broom-men, and takes use for them, would   165
  do't.
    [*Aside to Bracciano*] Hand her, my lord, and kiss her; be
    not like
  A ferret to let go your hold with blowing.
Bracciano. Let us renew right hands.
Vittoria.   Hence!   170
Bracciano. Never shall rage, or the forgetful wine,
  Make me commit like fault.
Flamineo. [*Aside to Bracciano*] Now you are i'th'way on't,
  follow't hard.
Bracciano. Be thou at peace with me; let all the world
  Threaten the cannon.   175
Flamineo. [*To Vittoria*]   Mark his penitence.
  Best natures do commit the grossest faults
  When they're giv'n o'er to jealousy, as best wine
  Dying makes strongest vinegar. I'll tell you;
  The sea's more rough and raging than calm rivers,   180
  But nor so sweet nor wholesome. A quiet woman
  Is a still water under a great bridge.
  A man may shoot her safely.
Vittoria. O ye dissembling men!
Flamineo.   We sucked that, sister,
  From women's breasts, in our first infancy.   185

---

164. *put out*] blinded (by your cruel denial).
166. *broom-men*] street-sweepers.
use] interest, usury.
168. *Hand*] touch.
169.] It was a superstition that blowing upon a ferret would make it
relinquish anything held in its teeth.
171. *forgetful*] inducing forgetfulness.
176. *Threaten the cannon*] i.e. threaten us with the use of force.
182. *a great bridge*] The Quarto edition of 1665 made the allusion obvious
by emending to 'London Bridge'; when tides ran high, it was difficult or
impossible to pass underneath, or 'shoot' this landmark bridge. Cf. proverb:
'London Bridge was made for wise men to go over and fools to go under'.

Vittoria. To add misery to misery.

Bracciano.   Sweetest—

Vittoria. Am I not low enough?
    Ay, ay, your good heart gathers like a snowball,
    Now your affection's cold.

Flamineo.   Ud's foot, it shall melt
    To a heart again, or all the wine in Rome   190
    Shall run o'th'lees for't.

Vittoria. Your dog or hawk should be rewarded better
    Than I have been. I'll speak not one word more.

Flamineo. Stop her mouth
    With a sweet kiss, my lord.   195
                    [*Bracciano embraces Vittoria.*]
    So, now the tide's turned the vessel's come about—
    He's a sweet armful. O we curled-haired men
    Are still most kind to women. This is well.

Bracciano. That you should chide thus!

Flamineo.   O, sir, your little chimneys
    Do ever cast most smoke. I sweat for you.   200
    Couple together with as deep a silence
    As did the Grecians in their wooden horse.
    My lord, supply your promises with deeds;
    You know that painted meat no hunger feeds.

Bracciano. Stay—ingrateful Rome!   205

Flamineo. Rome! It deserves to be called Barbary, for our
    villainous usage.

Bracciano. Soft; the same project which the Duke of Florence

---

188. *like a snowball*] i.e. like a snowball rolling and accumulating more snow. Vittoria implies, tauntingly, that Bracciano is acting on his better feelings now that he is no longer attracted to her sexually.

191. *o'th'lees*] down to the dregs.

192. *rewarded*] another hunting term; the 'reward' was part of the prey.

196. *come about*] changed course, heading into the current.

198. *still*] always, continually.

202. *their wooden horse*] i.e. the horse used to deceive Troy and bring Greek soldiers within the besieged city's walls.

203. *supply*] fulfil.

205. *ingrateful Rome*] the city was proverbially ungrateful to those who served it.

206-7. *for . . . usage*] for the villainous way it has treated us.

208. *project*] plan, scheme.

    (Whether in love or gullery I know not)
    Laid down for her escape, will I pursue.   210
Flamineo. And no time fitter than this night, my lord;
    The Pope being dead, and all the cardinals entered
    The conclave for th'electing a new Pope,
    The city in a great confusion,
    We may attire her in a page's suit,   215
    Lay her post-horse, take shipping, and amain
    For Padua.
Bracciano. I'll instantly steal forth the Prince Giovanni,
    And make for Padua. You two, with your old mother
    And young Marcello that attends on Florence,   220
    If you can work him to it, follow me.
    I will advance you all; for you Vittoria,
    Think of a duchess' title.
Flamineo.   Lo you, sister.
    Stay, my lord; I'll tell you a tale. The crocodile, which
    lives in the river Nilus, hath a worm breeds i'th'teeth of't, 225
    which puts it to extreme anguish. A little bird, no bigger
    than a wren, is barber-surgeon to this crocodile; flies into
    the jaws of't; picks out the worm; and brings present
    remedy. The fish, glad of ease but ingrateful to her that
    did it, that the bird may not talk largely of her abroad for 230
    non-payment, closeth her chaps intending to swallow
    her, and so put her to perpetual silence. But nature,
    loathing such ingratitude, hath armed this bird with a
    quill or prick on the head, top o'th'which wounds the
    crocodile i'th'mouth; forceth her open her bloody prison; 235
    and away flies the pretty tooth-picker from her cruel
    patient.
Bracciano. Your application is, I have not rewarded

---

209. *gullery*] craftiness.
216. *Lay*] station (on the way).
amain] at once, with all speed.
220. *Florence*] the Duke of Florence.
224–37.] This 'tale' could be found in several sources; Webster seems to
have taken it from Topsell, *History of Serpents* (1607–08).
225. *worm . . . of't*] a current explanation of toothache.
229. *fish*] The crocodile is a reptile, of course, but it is aquatic.
230. *largely*] openly, at length.

The service you have done me.

Flamineo.   No, my lord;
You, sister, are the crocodile; you are blemished in your   240
fame; my lord cures it. And though the comparison hold
not in every particle, yet observe, remember, what good
the bird with the prick i'th'head hath done you; and scorn
ingratitude.

[*Aside*] It may appear to some ridiculous   245
Thus to talk knave and madman, and sometimes
Come in with a dried sentence, stuffed with sage.
But this allows my varying of shapes:
Knaves do grow great by being great men's apes.

                                                Exeunt.

[IV. iii]

        Enter LODOVICO, GASPARO, *and six* Ambassadors.
        At another door [FRANCISCO] *the* Duke of Florence.

Francisco. So, my lord, I commend your diligence.
        Guard well the conclave, and, as the order is,
        Let none have conference with the cardinals.
Lodovico. I shall, my lord. Room for the ambassadors!
Gasparo. They're wondrous brave today. Why do they wear   5
        These several habits?
Lodovico.   O sir, they're knights
        Of several orders.
        That lord i'th'black cloak with the silver cross

---

241. *fame*] reputation.

243. *prick*] Flamineo, in his alternative application of the story, may use
the word to suggest a *double entendre*.

247. *sentence*] aphorism.

sage] (1) the herb; (2) wisdom; as at I.ii.136.

IV.iii.0.1.] The scene is located outside the Pope's palace in Rome, near
the Sistine Chapel.

0.2. At another door] Lodovico, assisted by Gasparo, has been supervising
the return of the ambassadors from the conclave for electing the new Pope;
Francisco has not been within the conclave. Dramatic time foreshortens
events so that one brief scene shows both the beginning and end of the
conclave.

5. *wondrous brave*] magnificently dressed.

Is Knight of Rhodes; the next Knight of St Michael;
That of the Golden Fleece; the Frenchman there   10
Knight of the Holy Ghost; my lord of Savoy
Knight of th'Annunciation; the Englishman
Is Knight of th'honoured Garter, dedicated
Unto their saint, St George. I could describe to you
Their several institutions, with the laws   15
Annexèd to their orders; but that time
Permits not such discovery.

Francisco.   Where's Count Lodowick?
Lodovico. Here, my lord.
Francisco.   'Tis o'th'point of dinner time.
Marshal the cardinals' service.
Lodovico.   Sir, I shall.

Enter Servants *with several dishes covered.*

Stand, let me search your dish.—Who's this for?   20
Servant. For my Lord Cardinal Monticelso.
Lodovico. Whose this?
Servant.   For my Lord Cardinal of Bourbon.
French Ambassador. Why doth he search the dishes?—to observe
What meat is dressed?
English Ambassador.   No sir, but to prevent
Lest any letters should be conveyed in   25

---

9. *Rhodes*] The order of the Knights of St John of Jerusalem was founded during the First Crusade; they had to move from Jerusalem to Rhodes, then to Crete, and finally to Malta; their robe had an eight-pointed silver cross (the Maltese Cross) embroidered on it.

St Michael] an order founded by Louis XI in 1469.

10. *Golden Fleece*] an order founded by Philip the Good, Duke of Burgundy, on his wedding day, 10 January 1430.

11. *Holy Ghost*] an order founded by Henry III in 1578, ranking above that of St Michael.

12. *Annunciation*] the order was founded by Amadeus VI of Savoy in 1362; its dress was of white satin with a cloak of purple velvet. As the most noble order in Italy, its representative should come last in the procession, but here the English knight has been given that prominence.

19. *Marshall . . . service*] Take charge of the servants waiting on the cardinals.

24. *meat*] food.
dressed] prepared.

To bribe or to solicit the advancement
Of any cardinal. When first they enter,
'Tis lawful for the ambassadors of princes
To enter with them, and to make their suit
For any man their prince affecteth best;   30
But after, till a general election,
No man may speak with them.
Lodovico. You that attend on the lord cardinals,
Open the window and receive their viands.

[*A* Conclavist *appears briefly at the window.*]

Conclavist. You must return the service; the lord cardinals   35
Are busied 'bout electing of the Pope.
They have given o'er scrutiny, and are fallen
To admiration.
Lodovico.   Away, away.
Francisco. I'll lay a thousand ducats you hear news
Of a Pope presently,—hark; sure he's elected,—   40

[*The*] Cardinal [of ARRAGON *appears*] *on the terrace.*

Behold! My lord of Arragon appears
On the church battlements.
*Arragon. Denuntio vobis gaudium magnum. Reverendissimus
    Cardinalis Lorenzo de Monticelso electus est in sedem
    apostolicam, et elegit sibi nomen Paulum Quartum.*   45
Omnes. Vivat Sanctus Pater Paulus Quartus.

[*Enter* Servant.]

---

30. *affecteth*] prefers.
34. *the window*] The Red Bull stage, where the play was first performed,
had windows and a balcony (see 'terrace', l. 40.1 below) overlooking the
main stage.
37. *scrutiny*] a technical term for examining votes at papal elections.
38. *admiration*] The correct word for this alternative way of proceeding
was 'adoration'; at least two-thirds of the cardinals had to turn towards a
single candidate and bow.
39. *lay*] wager.
43–6.] I bring you tidings of great joy. The Most Reverend Cardinal
Lorenzo di Monticelso has been elected to the Apostolic See, and has chosen
the title of Paul IV.—*All.* Long live the Holy Father, Paul IV. According to
Webster's source, the cardinal 'shows forth a cross' and then announces the
election 'with a loud voice'.

Servant. Vittoria, my lord—
Francisco.   Well; what of her?
Servant. Is fled the city—
Francisco.   Ha?
Servant.   With Duke Bracciano.
Francisco. Fled? Where's the prince Giovanni?
Servant.   Gone with his father.
Francisco. Let the matrona of the convertites   50
    Be apprehended. Fled—O, damnable!

                            [*Exit* Servant.]

    [*Aside*] How fortunate are my wishes. Why, 'twas this
    I only laboured. I did send the letter
    T'instruct him what to do. Thy fame, fond duke,
    I first have poisoned; directed thee the way   55
    To marry a whore; what can be worse? This follows:
    The hand must act to drown the passionate tongue;
    I scorn to wear a sword and prate of wrong.

                    Enter MONTICELSO *in state.*

*Monticelso. Concedimus vobis apostolicam benedictionem et
    remissionem peccatorum.*   [*Francisco whispers to him.*] 60
    My lord reports Vittoria Corombona
    Is stol'n from forth the house of convertites
    By Bracciano, and they're fled the city.
    Now, though this be the first day of our seat,
    We cannot better please the divine power   65
    Than to sequester from the holy church
    These cursèd persons. Make it therefore known,
    We do denounce excommunication
    Against them both; all that are theirs in Rome
    We likewise banish. Set on.   70

---

51. *apprehended*] arrested.
54. *fond*] infatuated, foolish.
57.] i.e. deeds must confirm passionate words.
58.1. *in state*] According to Webster's source, before the new Pope showed himself to the people, he was divested of his cardinal's robes and dressed as the pontiff, that is all in white. See Introduction on the play's use of colour symbolism.
59–60.] We grant you the Apostolic blessing and remission of sins.
64. *seat*] technical term for the throne and office of a Pope.
68. *denounce*] pronounce as sentence.

Exeunt [all except FRANCISCO *and* LODOVICO].

Francisco. Come, dear Lodovico.
   You have ta'en the sacrament to prosecute
   Th'intended murder.

Lodovico.   With all constancy.
   But, sir, I wonder you'll engage yourself
   In person, being a great prince.

Francisco.   Divert me not.   75
   Most of his court are of my faction,
   And some are of my counsel. Noble friend,
   Our danger shall be 'like in this design;
   Give leave part of the glory may be mine.

                         Exit FRANCISCO.

     [*Re*]*enter* MONTICELSO.

Monticelso. Why did the Duke of Florence with such care   80
   Labour your pardon? Say.

Lodovico. Italian beggars will resolve you that
   Who, begging of an alms, bid those they beg of
   Do good for their own sakes; or't may be
   He spreads his bounty with a sowing hand,   85
   Like kings, who many times give out of measure,
   Not for desert so much as for their pleasure.

Monticelso. I know you're cunning. Come, what devil was that
   That you were raising?

Lodovico.   Devil, my lord?

Monticelso.   I ask you
   How doth the duke employ you, that his bonnet   90
   Fell with such compliment unto his knee
   When he departed from you?

Lodovico.   Why, my lord,
   He told me of a resty Barbary horse

---

  82. *resolve*] explain to.

  83. *Who . . . alms*] whoever they are, when they ask for charity. Lodovico
mockingly suggests that it is not for him to suggest why Francisco worked to
achieve his pardon.

  86. *out of measure*] without discretion, excessively.

  88. *cunning*] (1) crafty, guileful; (2) possessing magical skill.

  93. *resty*] inactive, sluggish.

Which he would fain have brought to the career,
The 'sault, and the ring-galliard. Now, my lord,   95
I have a rare French rider.
Monticelso.   Take you heed,
Lest the jade break your neck. Do you put me off
With your wild horse-tricks? Sirrah, you do lie.
O, thou'rt a foul black cloud, and thou dost threat
A violent storm.
Lodovico.   Storms are i'th'air, my lord;   100
I am too low to storm.
Monticelso.   Wretched creature!
I know that thou art fashioned for all ill,
Like dogs, that once get blood, they'll ever kill.
About some murder? Was't not?
Lodovico.   I'll not tell you;
And yet I care not greatly if I do.—   105
Marry, with this preparation! Holy father,
I come not to you as an intelligencer,
But as a penitent sinner. What I utter
Is in confession merely, which you know
Must never be revealed.
Monticelso.   You have o'erta'en me.   110
Lodovico. Sir, I did love Bracciano's duchess dearly;
Or rather I pursued her with hot lust,
Though she ne'er knew on't. She was poisoned,
Upon my soul she was, for which I have sworn
T'avenge her murder.
Monticelso.   To the Duke of Florence?   115
Lodovico. To him I have.
Monticelso.   Miserable creature!

94–5. *career . . . ring-galliard*] exercises in the 'manage' of a horse.

96. *French rider*] The French were noted for horsemanship; see *The Duchess of Malfi*, I.i.141–2.

97. *jade*] (1) horse; (2) woman (contemptuous).

98. *horse-tricks*] (1) the exercises of the manage; (2) horse-play, improprieties, whore's tricks. Monticelso has recognized a line of sexual innuendo in Lodovico's talk of an imaginary horse.

106. *Marry*] i.e. indeed.

107. *intelligencer*] informer, spy.

110. *o'erta'en*] overreached, got the better of. (A priest told something in confession is obliged not to reveal or exploit his knowledge.)

If thou persist in this, 'tis damnable.
Dost thou imagine thou canst slide on blood
And not be tainted with a shameful fall?
Or like the black and melancholic yew tree,   120
Dost think to root thyself in dead men's graves,
And yet to prosper? Instruction to thee
Comes like sweet showers to over-hardened ground;
They wet, but pierce not deep. And so I leave thee
With all the Furies hanging 'bout thy neck,   125
Till by thy penitence thou remove this evil,
In conjuring from thy breast that cruel devil.
                                    Exit MONTICELSO.
Lodovico. I'll give it o'er. He says 'tis damnable;
     Besides I did expect his suffrage,
     By reason of Camillo's death.   130

          Enter Servant *and* FRANCISCO[, *and stand aside*].

Francisco. Do you know that count?
Servant.   Yes, my lord.
Francisco. Bear him these thousand ducats to his lodging;
     Tell him the Pope hath sent them. Happily
     That will confirm more than all the rest.   [*Exit.*]
Servant. Sir.   135
Lodovico. To me, sir?
Servant. His Holiness hath sent you a thousand crowns,
     And wills you if you travail, to make him
     Your patron for intelligence.
Lodovico.   His creature
     Ever to be commanded.   [*Exit* Servant.]   140
     Why now, 'tis come about. He railed upon me;
     And yet these crowns were told out and laid ready
     Before he knew my voyage. O the art,

---

119. *tainted*] (1) sullied, injured; (2) attainted, proved guilty.
129. *suffrage*] (1) approval, support; (2) prayers, intercessions.
132. *ducats*] In 1608, a ducat was reported to be worth 4s 8d in Venice; a
'crown' (see l. 137) would be only slightly more valuable.
133. *Happily*] haply, perhaps.
138. *travail*] go on a journey; statesmen often subsidized travel in order to
be provided with foreign news.
139. *His creature*] I am his humble servant.
142. *told*] counted.

The modest form of greatness! that do sit
Like brides at wedding dinners, with their looks turned   145
From the least wanton jests, their puling stomach
Sick of the modesty, when their thoughts are loose,
Even acting of those hot and lustful sports
Are to ensue about midnight; such his cunning!
He sounds my depth thus with a golden plummet,—   150
I am doubly armed now. Now to th'act of blood;
There's but three Furies found in spacious hell,
But in a great man's breast three thousand dwell.

                                        [*Exit.*]

[v. i]

A passage over the stage of BRACCIANO, FLAMINEO,
MARCELLO, HORTENSIO, [VITTORIA] COROMBONA,
            CORNELIA, ZANCHE *and others.*
      [FLAMINEO *and* HORTENSIO *remain.*]

Flamineo. In all the weary minutes of my life,
      Day ne'er broke up till now. This marriage
      Confirms me happy.
Hortensio.   'Tis a good assurance.
      Saw you not yet the Moor that's come to court?

---

144. *form*] often used for 'behaviour, manners', but with Webster it also
had the sense of 'merely outward appearance' (see *The Duchess of Malfi*,
I.i.156-7).

146. *puling*] unsettled, sickly.

147. *Sick of the modesty*] sick in pretended modesty.

148. *acting of*] performing, participating in (in their imaginations).

149. *Are*] that are.

152.] Some say (as in Webster's source for this couplet) that there are only
three Furies found in the whole of hell.

V.i.] Act V is located in Bracciano's palace in Padua.

0.3. *others*] These probably include the Ambassadors (cf. ll. 57-61 below); they would still be dressed as last seen at the Papal election only eighty
lines earlier, their robes bearing insignias of the Christian cross and the
Virgin Mary's sanctity. This pious display for the marriage of a proclaimed
whore and an excommunicate duke would reinforce Webster's repeated
comments on the power of great men and sycophancy of court society.

2. *up till*] until.

4. *the Moor*] i.e. Francisco in disguise.

Flamineo. Yes, and conferred with him i'th'duke's closet.   5
    I have not seen a goodlier personage,
    Nor ever talked with man better experienced
    In state affairs or rudiments of war.
    He hath, by report, served the Venetian
    In Candy these twice seven years, and been chief   10
    In many a bold design.
Hortensio.   What are those two
    That bear him company?
Flamineo. Two noblemen of Hungary, that living in the em-
    peror's service as commanders, eight years since, con-
    trary to the expectation of all the court entered into   15
    religion, into the strict order of Capuchins: but being not
    well settled in their undertaking they left their order and
    returned to court; for which, being after troubled in con-
    science, they vowed their service against the enemies of
    Christ; went to Malta; were there knighted; and in their   20
    return back, at this great solemnity, they are resolved for
    ever to forsake the world and settle themselves here in a
    house of Capuchins in Padua.
Hortensio. 'Tis strange.
Flamineo. One thing makes it so. They have vowed for ever to   25
    wear next their bare bodies those coats of mail they
    served in.
Hortensio. Hard penance. Is the Moor a Christian?
Flamineo. He is.
Hortensio. Why proffers he his service to our duke?   30
Flamineo. Because he understands there's like to grow
    Some wars between us and the Duke of Florence,
    In which he hopes employment.
    I never saw one in a stern bold look

---

5. *closet*] private chamber.

8. *rudiments*] principles (without the modern implication of 'rudimentary').

10. *Candy*] Crete.

12. *those two*] Lodovico and Gasparo; see n. 43.2 below.

16. *Capuchins*] an austere and poor order which branched off from the Franciscans about 1528; they did not become independent until 1619.

20. *knighted*] i.e. in the order of St John of Jerusalem (see IV.iii.9n.).

26. *coats of mail*] Hair shirts would be the normal austere garments; the metal would be 'Hard penance' indeed (l. 28).

Wear more command, nor in a lofty phrase   35
Express more knowing, or more deep contempt
Of our slight airy courtiers. He talks
As if he had travailed all the princes' courts
Of Christendom; in all things strives t'express
That all that should dispute with him may know   40
Glories, like glow-worms, afar off shine bright,
But, looked to near, have neither heat nor light.
The duke!

Enter BRACCIANO, [FRANCISCO Duke of] Florence *disguised like*
Mulinassar; LODOVICO, ANTONELLI, [*and*] GASPARO [*disguised,
and* another], *bearing their swords and helmets*[; CARLO *and* PEDRO].

Bracciano. You are nobly welcome. We have heard at full
   Your honourable service 'gainst the Turk.   45
   To you, brave Mulinassar, we assign
   A competent pension; and are inly sorrow
   The vows of these two worthy gentlemen
   Make them incapable of our proffered bounty.
   Your wish is you may leave your warlike swords   50
   For monuments in our chapel. I accept it
   As a great honour done me, and must crave
   Your leave to furnish out our duchess' revels.

---

41. *Glories*] fame, worldly honour and renown.

43.2. disguised] Lodovico and Gasparo are disguised as the two Capuchins.

43.3. *another*] in the Quarto named as Farnese; this is yet another 'ghost' character named in the original text but whom Webster abandoned without characterization (see II.i.0.2n.).

CARLO and PEDRO] included here on the strength of the Quarto's speech-prefixes ('Car.' and 'Ped.') at ll. 63 and 65 below; Pedro occurs in full at V.ii.17.1 and both are in full at V.vi.167.1–2. They are two of those in Bracciano's court who are of Francisco's 'faction' and 'counsel' (IV.iii.76–7); as such, they welcome their patron and the other three conspirators from Rome (ll. 63–7, below).

47. *competent*] adequate.

inly sorrow] grieved to the heart.

48. *these . . . gentlemen*] the (disguised) Capuchins, bound by a vow of poverty.

51. *monuments*] evidence, tokens (of their reformation and vows).

53. *furnish . . . revels*] contribute your presence to the revels designed to honour Vittoria.

Only one thing, as the last vanity
You e'er shall view: deny me not to stay   55
To see a barriers prepared tonight;
You shall have private standings. It hath pleased
The great ambassadors of several princes
In their return from Rome to their own countries
To grace our marriage, and to honour me   60
With such a kind of sport.

Francisco.   I shall persuade them
To stay, my lord.

Bracciano.   Set on there to the presence.

          Exeunt BRACCIANO, FLAMINEO, *and* [HORTENSIO].

Carlo. Noble my lord, most fortunately welcome;

                              The conspirators here embrace.

You have our vows sealed with the sacrament
To second your attempts.

Pedro.   And all things ready.   65
He could not have invented his own ruin,
Had he despaired, with more propriety.

Lodovico. You would not take my way.

Francisco.   'Tis better ordered.

Lodovico. T'have poisoned his prayer book, or a pair of beads,
The pommel of his saddle, his looking-glass,   70
Or th'handle of his racket—O that, that!
That while he had been bandying at tennis
He might have sworn himself to hell, and struck

---

54. *vanity*] worldly pleasure, expensive trifle.

56. *barriers*] see I.ii.29n.

57. *private standings*] special, reserved place from which to view.

62. *presence*] presence-chamber, throne room.

65. *second*] assist.

67. *propriety*] fitness.

69. *pair*] set.

70. *pommel . . . saddle*] Edward Squire was hanged in 1598, for trying to assassinate the Queen in this way; having touched the pommel, she would have conveyed the poison to her mouth and nostrils. Squire, like Webster's conspirators, had taken the sacrament to seal his vows to effect the murder.

73. *sworn . . . hell*] i.e. uttered profanities in exasperation at the game and then died in a sinful state.

His soul into the hazard! O my lord!
I would have our plot be ingenious,   75
And have it hereafter recorded for example
Rather than borrow example.
Francisco.   There's no way
More speeding than this thought on.
Lodovico.   On, then.
Francisco. And yet methinks that this revenge is poor,
Because it steals upon him like a thief,—   80
To have ta'en him by the casque in a pitched field,
Let him to Florence!
Lodovico.   It had been rare.—And there
Have crowned him with a wreath of stinking garlic,
T'have shown the sharpness of his government
And rankness of his lust. Flamineo comes.   85
                    Exeunt [all except FRANCISCO].

                    Enter FLAMINEO, MARCELLO, *and* ZANCHE.

Marcello. Why doth this devil haunt you? Say.
Flamineo.   I know not.
For, by this light, I do not conjure for her.
'Tis not so great a cunning as men think
To raise the devil, for here's one up already,
The greatest cunning were to lay him down.—   90
Marcello. She is your shame.
Flamineo.   I prithee pardon her.
In faith, you see, women are like to burs;

---

74. *soul . . . hazard*] The 'hasards' are openings in the inner wall of a royal
tennis court; to strike the ball into one of them is to win a stroke. Here there
is wordplay on *hazard* = 'peril, jeopardy'.

78. *speeding*] effective, successful.

81.] i.e. If only we could have captured him when ready for battle with his
tents pitched. (The *casque*, or headpiece of a helmet, was a symbol of military
authority.)

82. *rare*] a nonpareil.

84. *sharpness . . . government*] harshness of his conduct.

86. *devil*] i.e. the dark-skinned Zanche.

88. *cunning*] magic, occult art.

89–90. *up . . . lay him down*] with a suggestion of sexual excitment and
release.

92. *like to*] like.

burs] seed-heads which, proverbially, are likely to stick to clothes and hair,
etc.

Where their affection throws them, there they'll stick.

Zanche. That is my countryman, a goodly person;
When he's at leisure I'll discourse with him   95
In our own language.

Flamineo.   I beseech you do.—

Exit ZANCHE.

How is't, brave soldier? O that I had seen
Some of your iron days! I pray relate
Some of your service to us.

Francisco. 'Tis a ridiculous thing for a man to be his own   100
chronicle. I did never wash my mouth with mine own
praise for fear of getting a stinking breath.

Marcello. You're too stoical. The duke will expect other
discourse from you—

Francisco. I shall never flatter him. I have studied man too   105
much to do that; what difference is between the duke and
I? No more than between two bricks; all made of one
clay. Only't may be one is placed on the top of a turret,
the other in the bottom of a well by mere chance. If I were
placed as high as the duke, I should stick as fast, make as   110
fair a show, and bear out weather equally.

Flamineo. If this soldier had a patent to beg in churches, then
he would tell them stories.

Marcello. I have been a soldier too.

Francisco. How have you thrived?   115

Marcello. Faith, poorly.

Francisco. That's the misery of peace. Only outsides are then
respected; as ships seem very great upon the river, which
show very little upon the seas; so some men i'th' court
seem Colossuses in a chamber, who, if they came into the   120
field, would appear pitiful pigmies.

---

94. *my countryman*] i.e. 'Mulinassar'.

111. *fair*] Talking about himself, Francisco makes a quibbling allusion to
his disguise as the dark-skinned Mulinassar.

112. *patent to beg*] without a proper licence from a Justice of the Peace, a
beggar was liable to be whipped as a vagabond.

117. *misery of peace*] Soldiers returning from active service often com-
plained against the injustices and hardships of peacetime.

119. *show very little*] look tiny.

120. *Colossuses*] reference to the Colossus, a huge statue of the sun-god at
the harbour entrance of Rhodes.

Flamineo. Give me a fair room yet hung with arras, and some
    great cardinal to lug me by th'ears as his endeared
    minion.
Francisco. And thou may'st do the devil knows what villainy.   125
Flamineo. And safely.
Francisco. Right; you shall see in the country in harvest time,
    pigeons, though they destroy never so much corn, the
    farmer dare not present the fowling-piece to them. Why?
    Because they belong to the lord of the manor; whilst your   130
    poor sparrows that belong to the Lord of heaven, they go
    to the pot for't.
Flamineo. I will now give you some politic instruction. The
    duke says he will give you pension; that's but bare prom-
    ise; get it under his hand. For I have known men that   135
    have come from serving against the Turk; for three or
    four months they have had pension to buy them new
    wooden legs and fresh plasters; but after 'twas not to be
    had. And this miserable courtesy shows, as if a tormentor
    should give hot cordial drinks to one three-quarters dead   140
    o'th' rack, only to fetch the miserable soul again to en-
    dure more dog-days.

        Enter HORTENSIO, *a* young Lord, ZANCHE,
              and two more.

How now, gallants; what, are they ready for the barriers?
                             [*Exit* FRANCISCO.]
Young Lord. Yes; the lords are putting on their armour.
Hortensio. What's he?   145

---

122. *arras*] tapestry (a sign that the owner is wealthy). An arras was often
hung some distance from the wall or over a doorway or recess, and so
Flamineo probably implies that he could, if necessary, hide behind the
cardinal's.

123. *lug . . . ears*] i.e. fondle.

124. *minion*] darling, lover.

129. *fowling-piece*] shotgun.

132. *the pot*] the cooking pot.

135. *under his hand*] i.e. signed and sealed.

139. *miserable*] (1) compassionate; (2) miserly; with a further quibble at
l. 141.

140. *cordial*] heart-restoring.

142. *dog-days*] see III.ii.202n.

145. *he*] i.e. Francisco.

Flamineo. A new upstart: one that swears like a falc'ner, and
   will lie in the duke's ear day by day like a maker of
   almanacs; and yet I knew him since he came to th'court
   smell worse of sweat than an under-tennis-court-
   keeper.   150

Hortensio. Look you, yonder's your sweet mistress.

Flamineo. Thou art my sworn brother, I'll tell thee,—I do love
   that Moor, that witch, very constrainedly; she knows
   some of my villainy; I do love her, just as a man holds a
   wolf by the ears. But for fear of turning upon me, and   155
   pulling out my throat, I would let her go to the devil.

Hortensio. I hear she claims marriage of thee.

Flamineo. 'Faith, I made to her some such dark promise, and
   in seeking to fly from't I run on, like a frighted dog with
   a bottle at's tail, that fain would bite it off and yet dares 160
   not look behind him.—Now, my precious gipsy!

Zanche. Ay, your love to me rather cools than heats.

Flamineo. Marry, I am the sounder lover; we have many
   wenches about the town heat too fast.

Hortensio. What do you think of these perfumed gallants,   165
   then?

Flamineo. Their satin cannot save them. I am confident
   They have a certain spice of the disease,
   For they that sleep with dogs shall rise with fleas.

Zanche. Believe it! A little painting and gay clothes make you 170
   loathe me.

Flamineo. How? Love a lady for painting or gay apparel? I'll
   unkennel one example more for thee. Aesop had a foolish

---

148. *almanacs*] notoriously unreliable.

152. *sworn brother*] i.e. bound by oaths of friendship.

161. *gipsy*] alluding to her dark skin and, perhaps, her lust.

162. *your . . . heats*] i.e. your passion is fading; but Flamineo pretends that
Zanche is saying that he *cools*, or allays, her passion. Alternatively, in view of
'sounder' and 'disease' in following lines (ll. 163 and 168), he may mean that
by avoiding her he can avoid venereal disease.

167. *satin*] pun on 'Satan'.

168. *a certain spice*] i.e. some beginning of infection.

170–1. *A little . . . me*] i.e. Someone better dressed and made up than I has
won your love, so that now you hate me.

173–5. *Aesop . . . diners*] The point of the fable is the illusory quality of
physical attraction.

dog that let go the flesh to catch the shadow. I would have
courtiers be better diners.   175

Zanche. You remember your oaths.

Flamineo. Lovers' oaths are like mariners' prayers, uttered in
extremity; but when the tempest is o'er, and that the
vessel leaves tumbling, they fall from protesting to drinking. And yet amongst gentlemen protesting and drinking   180
go together, and agree as well as shoemakers and
Westphalia bacon. They are both drawers on; for drink
draws on protestation, and protestation draws on more
drink. Is not this discourse better now than the morality
of your sunburnt gentleman?   185

Enter CORNELIA.

Cornelia. Is this your perch, you haggard? Fly to th'stews.

                                         [*Strikes* ZANCHE.]

Flamineo. You should be clapped by th'heels now. Strike
i'th'court?   [*Exit* CORNELIA.]

Zanche. She's good for nothing but to make her maids
Catch cold a'nights; they dare not use a bed-staff,   190
For fear of her light fingers.

Marcello.   You're a strumpet,
An impudent one.   [*Kicks* ZANCHE.]

Flamineo.   Why do you kick her? Say,

---

178. *that*] when.

180. *protesting*] quarrelling (wordplay on use, at l. 179, meaning 'urgently praying').

181–2. *agree . . . bacon*] i.e. salt bacon draws men on to drink, and shoe-makers draw shoes on to feet.

185. *sunburnt gentleman*] i.e. Francisco, disguised as the dark-skinned Mulinassar.

186. *haggard*] wild (female) hawk; often used of a wild, intractable person and of a 'wanton'.

stews] brothels.

187. *clapped . . . heels*] put in irons or the stocks.

187–8. *Strike i'th'court*] Malicious striking which drew blood at the court of James I in England was an act of contempt, punishable by life imprison-ment, a fine, and the loss of the striker's right hand.

190. *bed-staff*] either a slat supporting the bedding or a staff used for beating up the bed in making it; here used quibblingly for (1) the man who should 'warm' the maids in bed; (2) a stick with which Cornelia could beat her maids.

Do you think that she's like a walnut tree?
Must she be cudgelled ere she bear good fruit?
Marcello. She brags that you shall marry her.
Flamineo.   What then?   195
Marcello. I had rather she were pitched upon a stake
  In some new-seeded garden, to affright
  Her fellow crows thence.
Flamineo.   You're a boy, a fool.
  Be guardian to your hound; I am of age.
Marcello. If I take her near you I'll cut her throat.   200
Flamineo. With a fan of feathers?
Marcello.   And for you—I'll whip
  This folly from you.
Flamineo.   Are you choleric?
  I'll purge't with rhubarb.
Hortensio.   O your brother!
Flamineo.   Hang him.
  He wrongs me most that ought t'offend me least.
  I do suspect my mother played foul play   205
  When she conceived thee.
Marcello.   Now by all my hopes,
  Like the two slaughtered sons of Oedipus,
  The very flames of our affection
  Shall turn two ways. Those words I'll make thee answer
  With thy heart blood.
Flamineo.   Do; like the geese in the progress,   210

---

194. *cudgelled*] Compare the proverb, 'A woman, a dog [or ass], and a
walnut tree: / The more you beat 'em, the better they be.'

201. *With . . . feathers?*] Flamineo mocks Marcello's threat of using his
sword.

202. *Are you choleric*] Flamineo enrages Marcello by treating his moral
indignation as a physical ailment (see next note).

203. *rhubarb*] a common purgative; see *The Duchess of Malfi*, II.v.12–13.

207–9. *Like . . . ways*] Eteocles and Polynices killed each other in single
combat for their father's throne; according to the usual account, when they
were burnt together on a pyre the flames parted as if their rivalry continued
after death. (Sophocles' *Antigone* treats the sons' burial very differently.)

210–11. *Do . . . me*] Royal progresses (see I.ii.176 and n) were known as
occasions for licentiousness; *geese* (= prostitutes) followed the court, and so
were readily available. Or Flamineo may merely be telling his brother to
follow him as one goose follows another.

You know where you shall find me.   [*Exit.*]
Marcello.   Very good.—
An thou beest a noble friend, bear him my sword,
And bid him fit the length on't.
Young Lord.   Sir, I shall.
                              [*Exeunt all but* ZANCHE.]

          Enter FRANCISCO *the* Duke of Florence [*disguised*
                    as Mulinassar].

Zanche. [*Aside*] He comes. Hence, petty thought of my
          disgrace!
          [*To him*] I ne'er loved my complexion till now,   215
          Cause I may boldly say, without a blush,
          I love you.
Francisco.   Your love is untimely sown;
          There's a spring at Michaelmas, but 'tis but a faint one.
          I am sunk in years, and I have vowed never to marry.
Zanche. Alas! Poor maids get more lovers than husbands; yet   220
          you may mistake my wealth. For, as when ambassadors
          are sent to congratulate princes there's commonly sent
          along with them a rich present, so that though the prince
          like not the ambassador's person nor words yet he likes
          well of the presentment; so I may come to you in the   225
          same manner and be better loved for my dowry than my
          virtue.
Francisco. I'll think on the motion.
Zanche. Do.—I'll now detain you no longer. At your better
          leisure I'll tell you things shall startle your blood.   230
          Nor blame me that this passion I reveal;
          Lovers die inward that their flames conceal.

---

    212. *An*] if.
    him] i.e. Flamineo.
    213. *fit . . . on't*] i.e. be ready to fight a duel.
    214. *my disgrace*] my shame in being the wooer.
    216. *Cause*] because.
    218. *Michaelmas*] 29 September (when, traditionally, an 'Indian summer'
can be expected).
    225. *presentment*] presentation, present.
    228. *motion*] proposal, offer.
    232. *flames*] i.e. passions of love (conventionally poetic).

Francisco. [*Aside*] Of all intelligence this may prove the best;
    Sure I shall draw strange fowl from this foul nest.

Exeunt.

[v.ii]

Enter MARCELLO and CORNELIA.

Cornelia. I hear a whispering all about the court
    You are to fight. Who is your opposite?
    What is the quarrel?
Marcello.   'Tis an idle rumour.
Cornelia. Will you dissemble? Sure you do not well
    To fright me thus; you never look thus pale   5
    But when you are most angry. I do charge you
    Upon my blessing.—Nay, I'll call the duke,
    And he shall school you.
Marcello.   Publish not a fear
    Which would convert to laughter; 'tis not so.
    Was not this crucifix my father's?
Cornelia.   Yes.   10
Marcello. I have heard you say, giving my brother suck,
    He took the crucifix between his hands

Enter FLAMINEO.

    And broke a limb off.
Cornelia.   Yes; but 'tis mended.
Flamineo. I have brought your weapon back.

FLAMINEO runs MARCELLO through.

Cornelia. ——   Ha, O my horror!
Marcello. You have brought it home indeed.
Cornelia.   Help! O, he's murdered.   15

---

233. *intelligence*] secret information.
234. *foul*] punning on 'fowl'.

V.ii.8. *Publish*] make public.
10. *this crucifix*] presumably one hanging round Cornelia's neck.
13. *broke . . . off*] an ominous sign of Flamineo's innate evil.
15. *home*] (1) all the way in; (2) to the family.

Flamineo. Do you turn your gall up? I'll to sanctuary,
    And send a surgeon to you.   [*Exit.*]

                Enter CARLO, HORTENSIO, PEDRO.

Hortensio.   How? O'th' ground?
Marcello. O mother, now remember what I told
    Of breaking off the crucifix:—farewell—
    There are some sins which heaven doth duly punish   20
    In a whole family. This it is to rise
    By all dishonest means. Let all men know
    That tree shall long time keep a steady foot
    Whose branches spread no wider than the root. [*Dies.*]
Cornelia. O my perpetual sorrow!
Hortensio.   Virtuous Marcello.   25
    He's dead. Pray leave him, lady; come, you shall.
Cornelia. Alas he is not dead; he's in a trance.
    Why, here's nobody shall get any thing by his death. Let
    me call him again, for God's sake.
Carlo. I would you were deceived.   30
Cornelia. O, you abuse me, you abuse me, you abuse me.
    How many have gone away thus for lack of tendance!
    Rear up's head, rear up's head; his bleeding inward will
    kill him.
Hortensio. You see he is departed.   35
Cornelia. Let me come to him; give me him as he is, if he be
    turned to earth; let me but give him one hearty kiss, and
    you shall put us both into one coffin; fetch a looking-
    glass, see if his breath will not stain it; or pull out some
    feathers from my pillow, and lay them to his lips. Will you   40
    lose him for a little pains-taking?
Hortensio. Your kindest office is to pray for him.
Cornelia. Alas! I would not pray for him yet. He may live to
    lay me i'th'ground, and pray for me, if you'll let me come
    to him.   45

---

16. *turn . . . up*] possibly a variant of 'to turn up one's heels'(= 'to die'); or
a reference to Marcello spitting up blood.

   to sanctuary] i.e. to a church where civil powers cannot arrest.

23–4.] a proverb warning against overweening ambition.

32. *gone away*] died.

37. *earth*] i.e. dust.

Enter BRACCIANO *all armed, save the beaver, with*
FLAMINEO[, FRANCISCO *disguised as* Mulinassar, *a* Page, *and*
LODOVICO *disguised*].

Bracciano. Was this your handiwork?
Flamineo. It was my misfortune.
Cornelia. He lies, he lies! He did not kill him; these have killed
    him, that would not let him be better looked to.
Bracciano. Have comfort, my grieved mother.   50
Cornelia. O, you screech-owl!
Hortensio. Forbear, good madam.
Cornelia. Let me go, let me go!
               She runs to FLAMINEO *with her knife drawn*
                    and coming to him lets it fall.
    The God of heaven forgive thee. Dost not wonder
    I pray for thee? I'll tell thee what's the reason: 55
    I have scarce breath to number twenty minutes;
    I'd not spend that in cursing. Fare thee well.
    Half of thyself lies there; and may'st thou live
    To fill an hour-glass with his mouldered ashes,
    To tell how thou shouldst spend the time to come   60
    In blest repentance.
Bracciano.   Mother, pray tell me
    How came he by his death? What was the quarrel?
Cornelia. Indeed, my younger boy presumed too much
    Upon his manhood; gave him bitter words;
    Drew his sword first; and so, I know not how,   65
    For I was out of my wits, he fell with's head
    Just in my bosom.
Page. This is not true, madam.
Cornelia.   I pray thee peace.

    45.1. beaver] helmet.
    50. *mother*] i.e. mother-in-law. (Cornelia indignantly rejects the title.)
    51. *screech-owl*] bird of ill omen.
    63–7.] Cornelia is trying to save Flamineo's life and put the blame on
Marcello by saying he drew first.
    63. *my younger boy*] Marcello.
    64. *him*] Flamineo.
    68. *This . . . madam*] The young voice of the Page accentuates the effective
contrast of this simple denial, especially after the pause indicated by the half-
line 67. This edition follows a third Quarto edition of 1665 in bringing the
Page on stage with Bracciano, but some editors direct him to enter at the
beginning of the scene so that he will be an eyewitness of the murder.

One arrow's grazed already; it were vain
T'lose this, for that will ne'er be found again.   70
Bracciano. Go, bear the body to Cornelia's lodging;
And we command that none acquaint our duchess
With this sad accident. For you, Flamineo,
Hark you, I will not grant your pardon.
Flamineo.   No?
Bracciano. Only a lease of your life. And that shall last   75
But for one day. Thou shalt be forced each evening
To renew it, or be hanged.
Flamineo.   At your pleasure.

> LODOVICO *sprinkles* BRACCIANO's
> *beaver with a poison.*

Your will is law now, I'll not meddle with it.
Bracciano. You once did brave me in your sister's lodging;
I'll now keep you in awe for't. Where's our beaver?   80
Francisco. [*Aside*] He calls for his destruction. Noble youth,
I pity thy sad fate. Now to the barriers.
This shall his passage to the black lake further:
The last good deed he did, he pardoned murther.

>   *Exeunt.*

[v.iii]

> *Charges and shouts. They fight at barriers;*
> *first single pairs, then three to three.*
> *Enter* BRACCIANO *and* FLAMINEO *with others* [*following,*
> *including* VITTORIA, GIOVANNI, *and* FRANCISCO
> *disguised as* Mulinassar].

Bracciano. An armourer! Ud's death, an armourer!

However the scene starts as a strictly private occasion (others enter only on hearing Marcello's death-cries); neither Cornelia nor Marcello would have a page in their service so that if he were on stage then it could be only as a spy. Evidently the point to be made is that Cornelia is so distressed and muddled that anyone could see that she *must* be lying.

69. *'s grazed*] i.e. (1) is lost in the grass; (2) has grazed (a reference to Marcello's wound). To find an arrow which is 'grassed', a second arrow is shot in the same direction to discover where the first would have fallen.

77.2. *beaver*] here used properly for the lower portion of the face-guard of a helmet.

82. *barriers*] See I.ii.29n.

83. *black lake*] Cocytus in the nether world; here a synonym for hell.

Flamineo. Armourer; where's the armourer?
Bracciano. Tear off my beaver.
Flamineo.   Are you hurt, my lord?
Bracciano. O, my brain's on fire,

Enter Armourer.

                     the helmet is poisoned!
Armourer. My lord, upon my soul—
Bracciano.   Away with him to torture.   5
                    [*Exit* Armourer, *guarded.*]
    There are some great ones that have hand in this,
    And near about me.
Vittoria.   O my loved lord! Poisoned?
Flamineo. Remove the bar; here's unfortunate revels.
    Call the physicians.

Enter two Physicians.

                    A plague upon you!
    We have too much of your cunning here already.   10
    I fear the ambassadors are likewise poisoned.
Bracciano. O I am gone already; the infection
    Flies to the brain and heart. O thou strong heart!
    There's such a covenant 'tween the world and it,
    They're loath to break.
Giovanni.   O my most lovèd father!   15
Bracciano. Remove the boy away,—
    Where's this good woman? Had I infinite worlds
    They were too little for thee. Must I leave thee?
    What say yon screech-owls, is the venom mortal?
Physicians. Most deadly.
Bracciano.   Most corrupted politic hangman!   20
    You kill without book; but your art to save
    Fails you as oft as great men's needy friends.
    I that have given life to offending slaves
    And wretched murderers, have I not power
    To lengthen mine own a twelve-month?   25

V.iii.8. *bar*] i.e.barriers.
21–2. *You . . . friends*] i.e. You are never at a loss how to kill, but your art
fails you when you have to save life, just as those who have benefited from
great men fail to return friendship in time of need.
    without book] from memory, routinely.

[*To Vittoria*] Do not kiss me, for I shall poison thee.
This unction is sent from the great Duke of Florence.
Francisco. Sir, be of comfort.
Bracciano. O thou soft natural death, that art joint-twin
　　To sweetest slumber, no rough-bearded comet　　　　　　　30
　　Stares on thy mild departure; the dull owl
　　Beats not against thy casement; the hoarse wolf
　　Scents not thy carrion. Pity winds thy corse,
　　Whilst horror waits on princes.
Vittoria. I am lost for ever.　　　　　　　　　　　　　　　35
Bracciano. How miserable a thing it is to die
　　'Mongst women howling!

　　　　　[*Enter* LODOVICO *and* GASPARO, *in the habit of*
　　　　　　　　　　　Capuchins.]

　　　　　　　　　　What are those?
Flamineo.　　　　　　　　　　　　　　Franciscans.
　　They have brought the extreme unction.
Bracciano. On pain of death, let no man name death to me,
　　It is a word infinitely terrible.—　　　　　　　　　　40
　　Withdraw into our cabinet.

　　　　　　　　Exeunt [all] *but* FRANCISCO *and* FLAMINEO.
Flamineo. To see what solitariness is about dying princes. As
　　heretofore they have unpeopled towns, divorced friends,
　　and made great houses unhospitable, so now, O justice!
　　where are their flatterers now? Flatterers are but the　　45
　　shadows of princes' bodies; the least thick cloud makes
　　them invisible.
Francisco. There's great moan made for him.
Flamineo. 'Faith, for some few hours salt water will run most

---

27. *unction*] (1) medicine; (2) poison; (3) extreme unction.

29–30. *death . . . slumber*] a rephrasing of the proverb 'Sleep is the brother of death'.

30. *rough-bearded comet*] wild and fiery comet (an omen of disaster).

33. *winds thy corse*] wraps your corpse in grave-clothes.

34. *waits on*] attends, serves.

37. *Franciscans*] ironic: the supposed Capuchins (a branch of the Franciscan order) are in fact servants of Francisco.

41. *cabinet*] private apartment, room.

plentifully in every office o'th'court. But believe it: most   50
of them do but weep over their stepmothers' graves.
Francisco. How mean you?
Flamineo. Why? They dissemble, as some men do that live
within compass o'th'verge.
Francisco. Come, you have thrived well under him.   55
Flamineo. 'Faith, like a wolf in a woman's breast; I have been
fed with poultry; but for money, understand me, I had as
good a will to cozen him as e'er an officer of them all. But
I had not cunning enough to do it.
Francisco. What didst thou think of him? 'Faith, speak freely.   60
Flamineo. He was a kind of statesman, that would sooner have
reckoned how many cannon-bullets he had discharged
against a town, to count his expense that way, than how
many of his valiant and deserving subjects he lost before
it.   65
Francisco. O, speak well of the duke.
Flamineo. I have done. Wilt hear some of my court wisdom?

Enter LODOVICO [*disguised as before*].

To reprehend princes is dangerous; and to over-com-
mend some of them is palpable lying.
Francisco. How is it with the duke?
Lodovico.   Most deadly ill.   70
He's fall'n into a strange distraction.
He talks of battles and monopolies,
Levying of taxes, and from that descends
To the most brain-sick language. His mind fastens
On twenty several objects, which confound   75
Deep sense with folly. Such a fearful end

---

51. *over . . . graves*] i.e. hypocritically, as for an unloved stepmother.

53. *some men*] an ironical understatement.

54. *verge*] area within twelve miles of the king's court and so under the jurisdiction of the lord high steward.

56. *wolf*] ulcerous sore; because it was seen to consume the body's flesh, physicians used to feed it daily with fresh meat or poultry.

57. *poultry*] with pun on *paltry* = 'rubbish, trash'.

58. *cozen*] cheat.

64–5. *before it*] in front of the beseiged town.

71. *He's . . . distraction*] i.e. Bracciano is so crazed that he leaps from one subject to another.

May teach some men that bear too lofty crest,
Though they live happiest, yet they die not best.
He hath conferred the whole state of the dukedom
Upon your sister, till the prince arrive   80
At mature age.

Flamineo.   There's some good luck in that yet.
Francisco. See, here he comes.

Enter BRACCIANO, *presented in a bed,* VITTORIA *and others*[,
including GASPARO, *disguised as before*].

          There's death in's face already.
Vittoria. O my good lord!
Bracciano.   Away! You have abused me.
          These speeches are several kinds of distractions
                    and in the action should appear so.
You have conveyed coin forth our territories;
Bought and sold offices; oppressed the poor,   85
And I ne'er dreamt on't. Make up your accounts;
I'll now be mine own steward.

Flamineo.   Sir, have patience.
Bracciano. Indeed, I am too blame.
For, did you ever hear the dusky raven
Chide blackness? Or was't ever known the devil   90
Railed against cloven creatures?

Vittoria.   O, my lord!
Bracciano. Let me have some quails to supper.
Flamineo.   Sir, you shall.
Bracciano. No; some fried dog-fish. Your quails feed on
          poison,—
          That old dog-fox, that politician Florence,—

---

79. *state*] possessions, power, and dignity.
80. *your sister*] Vittoria.
the prince] Giovanni, now Vittoria's stepson.
82.1. presented in a bed] A bed is thrust forth on stage with Bracciano in
it.
84.] a serious offence.
88. *blame*] blameworthy.
92. *quails*] a great delicacy (and said, erroneously, to feed on poison); also
used = 'prostitutes'.
93. *dog-fish*] large, coarse fish, a small shark; used offensively of persons.
94. *Florence*] the Duke of Florence.

I'll forswear hunting and turn dog-killer;   95
Rare! I'll be friends with him; for mark you, sir, one dog
Still sets another a-barking. Peace, peace,
Yonder's a fine slave come in now.
Flamineo.   Where?
Bracciano.   Why, there.
In a blue bonnet, and a pair of breeches
With a great codpiece. Ha, ha, ha,   100
Look you his codpiece is stuck full of pins
With pearls o'th'head of them. Do not you know him?
Flamineo. No, my lord.
Bracciano.   Why, 'tis the devil.
I know him by a great rose he wears on's shoe
To hide his cloven foot. I'll dispute with him.   105
He's a rare linguist.
Vittoria.   My lord, here's nothing.
Bracciano. Nothing? Rare! Nothing! When I want money,
Our treasury is empty; there is nothing.—
I'll not be used thus.
Vittoria.   O! Lie still, my lord—
Bracciano. See, see, Flamineo that killed his brother   110
Is dancing on the ropes there; and he carries
A money-bag in each hand, to keep him even,
For fear of breaking's neck. And there's a lawyer
In a gown whipt with velvet, stares and gapes
When the money will fall. How the rogue cuts capers!   115
It should have been in a halter.
'Tis there; what's she?
Flamineo.   Vittoria, my lord.

---

95. *dog-killer*] Men were hired to kill stray or mad dogs in towns.
96. *Rare!*] How fine!
97. *Still*] always.
98. *slave*] rascal, menial servant.
101. *codpiece . . . pins*] a fashion of the time.
104. *rose*] rosette, or knot of ribbons.
106. *rare linguist*] good or voluble talker.
111. *ropes*] tightropes. (The raving Bracciano is fantasizing about danger and need.)
114. *whipt*] trimmed.
115. *When . . . fall*] to see when (1) Flamineo drops the money-bags; (2) payment is due.
116.] quibbling on 'dancing on the ropes' (l. 111 above).

Bracciano. Ha, ha, ha. Her hair is sprinkled with arras pow-
    der, that makes her look as if she had sinned in the pastry.
    What's he?   120

Flamineo. A divine, my lord.

Bracciano. He will be drunk. Avoid him; th'argument is fear-
    ful when churchmen stagger in't.
    Look you, six grey rats that have lost their tails
    Crawl up the pillow. Send for a rat-catcher.   125
    I'll do a miracle: I'll free the court
    From all foul vermin. Where's Flamineo?

Flamineo. I do not like that he names me so often,
    Especially on's death-bed; 'tis a sign
    I shall not live long. See, he's near his end.   130

                  BRACCIANO *seems here near his end.*
                LODOVICO *and* GASPARO *in the habit of*
                      Capuchins present him in his bed
                      with a crucifix and hallowed candle.

Lodovico. Pray give us leave. *Attende Domine Bracciane—*

Flamineo. See, see, how firmly he doth fix his eye
    Upon the crucifix.

Vittoria.   O, hold it constant.
    It settles his wild spirits; and so his eyes
    Melt into tears.   135

Lodovico. (*by the crucifix*) *Domine Bracciane, solebas in bello*
    tutus esse tuo clypeo, nùnc hunc clypeum hosti tuo opponas
    infernali.

    118–19. *hair . . . powder*] Powdered orris, or iris, root was used for whiten-
ing and perfuming hair.

    119. *pastry*] place where pastry is made. (Bracciano imagines Vittoria
serving her lust there.)

    122. *drunk*] Webster makes the mad priest in *The Duchess of Malfi* cry, 'He
that drinks but to satisfy nature is damned' (IV.ii.96–7).

    123. *stagger*] hesitate; with pun on drunken behaviour.

    124. *six . . . tails*] i.e. witches (said to turn themselves into any animal they
pleased, except that the tail would always be missing).

    131.] Attende Domine Bracciane] Listen, Lord Bracciano.

    136–47. Domine . . . laevum] i.e. Lord Bracciano, you were accustomed
to be guarded in battle by your shield; now this shield [i.e. the crucifix] you
shall oppose against your infernal enemy.—Once with your spear you pre-
vailed in battle; now this holy spear [i.e. the hallowed taper] you shall wield
against the enemy of souls.—Listen, Lord Bracciano, if you now also approve
what has been enacted between us, turn your head to the right.—Rest

Gasparo. (*by the hallowed taper*) *Olim hastâ valuisti in bello;*
　　nùnc hanc sacram hastam vibrabis contra hostem animarum.　140
Lodovico. Attende Domine Bracciane si nunc quòque probas ea
　　quae acta sunt inter nos, flecte caput in dextrum.
Gasparo. Esto securus Domine Bracciane: cogita quantum habeas
　　meritorum—denique memineris meam animam pro tua
　　oppignoratam si quid esset periculi.　　　　　　　　　　145
Lodovico. Si nùnc quoque probas ea quae acta sunt inter nos, flecte
　　caput in laevum.
　　He is departing; pray stand all apart,
　　And let us only whisper in his ears
　　Some private meditations, which our order　　　　　　　150
　　Permits you not to hear.
　　　　　　　　　　Here the rest being departed LODOVICO
　　　　　　　　　　and GASPARO *discover themselves.*
Gasparo.　　　　　　　　　Bracciano!
Lodovico. Devil Bracciano. Thou art damned.
Gasparo.　　　　　　　　　　　　　　Perpetually.
Lodovico. A slave condemned and given up to the gallows
　　Is thy great lord and master.
Gasparo.　　　　　　　　　True; for thou
　　Art given up to the devil.
Lodovico.　　　　　　　　O, you slave!　　　　　　155
　　You that were held the famous politician;
　　Whose art was poison.
Gasparo.　　　　　　　　And whose conscience murder.
Lodovico. That would have broke your wife's neck down the
　　stairs

---

assured, Lord Bracciano; think how many good deeds you have done; lastly
remember that my soul is pledged for yours if there should be any peril.—If
you now also approve what has been enacted between us, turn your head to
the left.

　　This whole passage is taken from Erasmus' colloquy, *Funus*, a comparison
between the death of a good Christian and Georgius Balearicus who, 'trust-
ing to his wealth, sought by purchase to retain his standing beyond the
grave'. When the dying were speechless, it was customary for priests to ask
for signs of their faith.

　　158–9. *broke . . . poisoned*] possibly an allusion to reports that the Earl of
Leicester tried in 1560 to poison his wife, Amy Robsart, and then killed her
by having her thrown down the stairs, at the foot of which she was found
dead.

Ere she was poisoned

Gasparo.   That had your villainous sallets—

Lodovico. And fine embroidered bottles, and perfumes   160
Equally mortal with a winter plague—

Gasparo. Now there's mercury—

Lodovico.   And copperas—

Gasparo.   And quicksilver—

Lodovico. With other devilish pothecary stuff
A-melting in your politic brains. Dost hear?

Gasparo. This is Count Lodovico.

Lodovico.   This Gasparo.   165
And thou shalt die like a poor rogue.

Gasparo.   And stink
Like a dead fly-blown dog.

Lodovico.   And be forgotten
Before thy funeral sermon.

Bracciano.   Vittoria?
Vittoria!

Lodovico.   O the cursèd devil,
Come to himself again! We are undone.   170

Enter VITTORIA *and the* Attendants.

Gasparo. [*Aside*] Strangle him in private.
[*Aloud*] What? Will you call him again
To live in treble torments? For charity,
For Christian charity, avoid the chamber.

[*Exeunt* VITTORIA *etc.*]

Lodovico. You would prate, sir. This is a true-love knot   175
Sent from the Duke of Florence.

BRACCIANO *is strangled.*

Gasparo.   What—is it done?

---

159. *sallets*] salads; see IV.ii.61.

161. *mortal*] deadly.

winter plague] In England the plague was commonly most dangerous in
summertime; only the most virulent outbreaks thrived in winter.

162. *mercury*] In view of 'quicksilver' in the same line, Gasparo may refer
to the poisonous plant, *Mercurialis perennis* or 'wild mercury'; or he may
consciously repeat himself, concerned only to terrify Bracciano with words.

copperas] copper sulphate (mortally poisonous only when taken in considerable quantity).

167. *fly-blown*] maggot-infested.

174. *avoid*] clear.

Lodovico. The snuff is out. No woman-keeper i'th'world,
   Though she had practised seven year at the pest-house,
   Could have done't quaintlier.—My lords, he's dead.

        [*Re-enter* VITTORIA, FRANCISCO, *and* FLAMINEO,
            with Attendants.]

Omnes. Rest to his soul.
Vittoria.   O me! This place is hell.   180
           Exit VITTORIA[, *followed by all except*
         LODOVICO, FRANCISCO, *and* FLAMINEO].
Francisco. How heavily she takes it.
Flamineo.   O yes, yes;
   Had women navigable rivers in their eyes
   They would dispend them all. Surely I wonder
   Why we should wish more rivers to the city,
   When they sell water so good cheap. I'll tell thee,   185
   These are but moonish shades of griefs or fears;
   There's nothing sooner dry than women's tears.
   Why, here's an end of all my harvest; he has given me
      nothing—
   Court promises! Let wise men count them curst,
   For while you live he that scores best pays worst.   190
Francisco. Sure, this was Florence' doing.
Flamineo.   Very likely.
   Those are found weighty strokes which come from
      th'hand,

---

177. *snuff*] burning candle-wick, here betokening life.
  woman-keeper] female nurse; nurses were often suspected of killing off their patients.
  178. *the pest-house*] In 1594, the City of London built a pest-house, or hospital, for the confinement of those sick of the plague.
  179. *quaintlier*] more skilfully, cleverly.
  My lords] addressed to those entering.
  183. *dispend*] expend.
  184.] an allusion to Sir Hugh Middleton's 'New River', bringing fresh water thirty-nine miles from Ware to Islington. This ambitious and widely welcomed scheme was not in operation when this play was first performed; work had started in 1609, but was not finished until Michaelmas 1613.
  185. *good cheap*] cheaply.
  186. *moonish*] changeable, fickle.
  189. *them*] themselves.
  190. *scores*] runs up a score or debt, obtains on credit.
  192–3.] i.e. Cunning is more deadly than brute force. (Francisco has consistently preferred cunning throughout.)

But those are killing strokes which come from th'head.
O, the rare tricks of a Machivillian!
He doth not come like a gross plodding slave   195
And buffet you to death. No, my quaint knave,
He tickles you to death; makes you die laughing;
As if you had swallowed down a pound of saffron—
You see the feat—'tis practised in a trice
To teach court-honesty it jumps on ice.   200

Francisco. Now have the people liberty to talk
And descant on his vices.

Flamineo.   Misery of princes,
That must of force be censured by their slaves!
Not only blamed for doing things are ill,
But for not doing all that all men will.   205
One were better be a thresher.
Ud's death, I would fain speak with this duke yet.

Francisco. Now he's dead?

Flamineo. I cannot conjure; but if prayers or oaths
Will get to th'speech of him, though forty devils   210
Wait on him in his livery of flames,
I'll speak to him, and shake him by the hand,
Though I be blasted.   *Exit* FLAMINEO.

Francisco.   Excellent Lodovico!

---

194. *Machivillian*] Machiavellian; the Quarto's spelling is retained, for the
metre and for the pun on 'villain' (in line with the contemporary reputation
of the Italian politician).

196. *quaint*] skilled, ingenious.

198. *saffron*] Gerard's *Herbal* (1597) noted that taken in small quantities
it 'maketh a man merry'; other authorities added that taken in large doses it
could be fatal.

199–200.] You see the trick of a Machiavellian: it is carried out in a
moment and so teaches that honesty at court is always in peril.

court-honesty] the false honesty of a courtier.

202. *descant*] comment, enlarge. (A musical term signifying embroidery.)

203. *of force*] necessarily.

slaves] retainers, social inferiors.

204. *are ill*] that are evil.

205. *that*] that which.

will] wish, crave (them to do).

206. *thresher*] referred to as a 'filthy' occupation, along with thatchers and
sow-gelders, in Webster and Dekker's *Westward Ho!* (1605).

211. *Wait*] attend.

213. *blasted*] (1) discredited; (2) struck by heaven's wrath, hell-fire.

What? Did you terrify him at the last gasp?

Lodovico. Yes, and so idly, that the duke had like   215
T'have terrified us.

Francisco.   How?

Enter [ZANCHE] *the Moor.*

Lodovico.   You shall hear that hereafter.—
[*Aside*] See! Yon's the infernal, that would make up sport.
Now to the revelation of that secret
She promised when she fell in love with you.

Francisco. [*To Zanche*] You're passionately met in this sad
world.   220

Zanche. I would have you look up, sir; these court tears
Claim not your tribute to them. Let those weep
That guiltily partake in the sad cause.
I knew last night by a sad dream I had
Some mischief would ensue; yet to say truth   225
My dream most concerned you.

Lodovico.   Shall's fall a-dreaming?

Francisco. Yes, and for fashion sake I'll dream with her.

Zanche. Methought sir, you came stealing to my bed.

Francisco. Wilt thou believe me, sweeting? By this light,
I was a-dreamt on thee too; for methought   230
I saw thee naked.

Zanche.   Fie sir! As I told you,
Methought you lay down by me.

Francisco.   So dreamt I;
And, lest thou shouldst take cold, I covered thee
With this Irish mantle.

Zanche.   Verily, I did dream

---

215. *idly*] carelessly, ineffectually.
215–16. *had like T'have*] almost.
217. *infernal*] i.e. spirit of darkness (a scornful allusion to her skin-colour).
make up sport] have some fun.
221–2. *these . . . them*] you have no call to pretend to weep.
226. *Shall's*] shall we.
227. *fashion*] form's.
234. *Irish mantle*] plaid or blanket, often worn in rural Ireland without other clothing; so Francisco implies he was naked under it.

You were somewhat bold with me; but to come to't.   235
Lodovico. How? How? I hope you will not go to't here.
Francisco. Nay, you must hear my dream out.
Zanche.   Well, sir, forth.
Francisco. When I threw the mantle o'er thee, thou didst
     laugh
     Exceedingly, methought.
Zanche.   Laugh?
Francisco.   And cried'st out,
     The hair did tickle thee.
Zanche.   There was a dream indeed.   240
Lodovico. Mark her, I prithee; she simpers like the suds
     A collier hath been washed in.
Zanche. Come, sir; good fortune tends you; I did tell you
     I would reveal a secret. Isabella,
     The Duke of Florence' sister, was empoisoned   245
     By a 'fumed picture; and Camillo's neck
     Was broke by damned Flamineo; the mischance
     Laid on a vaulting-horse.
Francisco.   Most strange!
Zanche.   Most true.
Lodovico. The bed of snakes is broke.
Zanche. I sadly do confess I had a hand   250
     In the black deed.
Francisco.   Thou kept'st their counsel—
Zanche.   Right,
     For which, urged with contrition, I intend
     This night to rob Vittoria.
Lodovico.   Excellent penitence!
     Usurers dream on't while they sleep out sermons.
Zanche. To further our escape, I have entreated   255
     Leave to retire me, till the funeral,

---

235. *come to't*] (1) get on with my dream; (2) get on with it sexually.
Lodovico replies in the next line with a sexual joke about *going to it*, having
sex.
241–2. *simpers . . . in*] i.e. is obviously enjoying filthier jokes than anyone
else.
246. *'fumed*] perfumed.
249. *bed*] nest, tangled knot.
254.] Pious-seeming usurers dream of such a false penitence.

Unto a friend i'th'country. That excuse
Will further our escape. In coin and jewels
I shall, at least, make good unto your use
An hundred thousand crowns.

Francisco.   O noble wench!   260

Lodovico. Those crowns we'll share.

Zanche.   It is a dowry,
Methinks, should make that sunburnt proverb false,
And wash the Ethiop white.

Francisco.   It shall. Away!

Zanche. Be ready for our flight.

Francisco.   An hour 'fore day.

                    Exit [ZANCHE] *the Moor.*

O strange discovery! Why, till now we knew not   265
The circumstance of either of their deaths.

                    [*Re-*]*enter* [ZANCHE *the*] *Moor.*

Zanche. You'll wait about midnight in the chapel.

Francisco.   There.

                    [*Exit* ZANCHE.]

Lodovico. Why, now our action's justified,—

Francisco.   Tush for justice.
What harms it justice? We now, like the partridge,
Purge the disease with laurel; for the fame   270
Shall crown the enterprise and quit the shame. *Exeunt.*

[v. iv]

                    Enter FLAMINEO *and* GASPARO *at one door, another*
                    way GIOVANNI *attended.*

Gasparo. The young duke; did you e'er see a sweeter prince?

---

257. *Unto . . . country*] a casual excuse.

262. *sunburnt*] (1) familiar; (2) dark (appropriate to the dark-skinned, like
their two selves).

263. *And . . . white*] and make a black complexion seem white; perhaps
Francisco enjoys thinking that his own dark skin could indeed be washed
white.

269–71. *like . . . shame*] i.e. let the honour of the end justify the shameful-
ness of the means; with wordplay on *laurel* as a symbol of 'fame' and as a
medicine. (Pliny reports that partridges, doves etc. ate laurel as a purgative.)
quit] clear, pay off.

Flamineo. I have known a poor woman's bastard better fa-
voured. This is behind him; now, to his face all comparisons were hateful. Wise was the courtly peacock, that,
being a great minion, and being compared for beauty, by   5
some dottrels that stood by, to the kingly eagle, said the
eagle was a far fairer bird than herself, not in respect of
her feathers, but in respect of her long tallants. His will
grow out in time,—
    My gracious lord.   10
Giovanni. I pray leave me, sir.
Flamineo. Your grace must be merry. 'Tis I have cause to
mourn, for wot you what said the little boy that rode
behind his father on horseback?
Giovanni. Why, what said he?   15
Flamineo. 'When you are dead, father', said he, 'I hope then
I shall ride in the saddle.'—O, 'tis a brave thing for a man
to sit by himself! He may stretch himself in the stirrups,
look about, and see the whole compass of the
hemisphere. You're now, my lord, i'th'saddle.   20
Giovanni. Study your prayers, sir, and be penitent.
    'Twere fit you'd think on what hath former been;
    I have heard grief named the eldest child of sin.
                    Exit GIOVANNI [*and all except* FLAMINEO].
Flamineo. Study my prayers? He threatens me divinely;
    I am falling to pieces already. I care not, though, like   25
    Anacharsis, I were pounded to death in a mortar. And yet

V.iv.3. *behind him*] said behind Giovanni's back.

4. *were hateful*] would be undesirable, insulting.

6. *dottrels*] a species of plover; often used = 'simpletons', because the bird was supposed to imitate the fowler and so be easy game.

8. *tallants*] a sixteenth- to seventeenth-century form of both 'talons' and 'talents'; so Flamineo says that one must flatter a great person because he has the talent, or ability, to strike, as with an eagle's talons.

His] i.e. Giovanni's talons.

13. *wot*] know.

22.] You would do well to concentrate on what has happened already (not on future possibilities).

26. *Anarcharsis*] a Thracian prince of the sixth century B.C., who was renowned for his wisdom. Webster was ill-informed: it was Anaxarchus who was 'pounded to death in a mortar' by order of Nicocreon of whom he had spoken despitefully in front of Alexander. In Webster's source, Anacharsis was said to have been so virtuous that he 'jested at death' while being killed in this gruesome way.

that death were fitter for usurers' gold and themselves to
be beaten together, to make a most cordial cullis for the
devil.

He hath his uncle's villainous look already,   30

Enter Courtier.

In *decimo-sexto*.—Now sir, what are you?

Courtier. It is the pleasure sir, of the young duke
    That you forbear the presence, and all rooms
    That owe him reverence.

Flamineo.   So, the wolf and the raven   35
    Are very pretty fools when they are young.
    Is it your office, sir, to keep me out?

Courtier. So the duke wills.

Flamineo. Verily, master courtier, extremity is not to be used
    in all offices. Say that a gentlewoman were taken out   40
    of her bed about midnight, and committed to Castle
    Angelo, to the tower yonder, with nothing about her, but
    her smock; would it not show a cruel part in the gentle-
    man porter to lay claim to her upper garment, pull it o'er
    her head and ears, and put her in naked?   45

Courtier. Very good; you are merry.   [*Exit.*]

Flamineo. Doth he make a court ejectment of me? A flaming
    firebrand casts more smoke without a chimney than
    within't. I'll smoor some of them.

Enter [FRANCISCO Duke of] Florence[, *disguised*
as Mulinassar].

How now? Thou art sad.   50

Francisco. I met even now with the most piteous sight.

---

28. *cullis*] broth (in this case, a broth made by pounding up a usurer and
his gold in a pestle; so playing on *mortar*, l. 26).

31. decimo-sexto] size of a small book, of which each leaf is one-sixteenth
of a full sheet of paper.

33. *presence*] presence-chamber, throne room.

39. *extremity*] extreme rigour.

41-2. *Castle Angelo*] i.e. Castel Sant'Angelo at Rome; the real-life Vittoria
was imprisoned here for a time.

42. *tower yonder*] equating Castle Angelo with the Tower of London, for
Webster's London audience; see also V.vi.266.

47-8. *flaming firebrand*] probably with wordplay on Flamineo's own
name.

49. *smoor*] smother, suffocate.

Flamineo. Thou met'st another here—a pitiful
    Degraded courtier.
Francisco.   Your reverend mother
    Is grown a very old woman in two hours.
    I found them winding of Marcello's corse;   55
    And there is such a solemn melody
    'Tween doleful songs, tears, and sad elegies—
    Such as old grandames, watching by the dead,
    Were wont t'outwear the nights with—that, believe me,
    I had no eyes to guide me forth the room,   60
    They were so o'ercharged with water.
Flamineo.   I will see them.
Francisco. 'Twere much uncharity in you; for your sight
    Will add unto their tears.
Flamineo.   I will see them.
    They are behind the traverse. I'll discover
    Their superstitious howling. [*Draws the traverse curtain.*]   65

    CORNELIA, [ZANCHE] the Moor *and three other* Ladies
        discovered, winding MARCELLO'*s corse.*
                        A song.

Cornelia. This rosemary is withered, pray get fresh;
    I would have these herbs grow up in his grave
.   When I am dead and rotten. Reach the bays;
    I'll tie a garland here about his head;
    'Twill keep my boy from lightning. This sheet   70
    I have kept this twenty year, and every day
    Hallowed it with my prayers. I did not think
    He should have wore it.
Zanche.   Look you, who are yonder?
Cornelia. O, reach me the flowers.

---

64. *traverse*] screen or curtain across a room, hall, or stage.
65.2. discovered] implied by 'discover', l. 64.
66ff.] The imitation of Shakespeare's Ophelia (*Hamlet*, IV.v) is so close
that an echo of that scene might well have been intended, to set an appropriate tone and, by contrast, to accentuate Cornelia's age.
66. *rosemary*] The evergreen herb was an emblem of immortality; used as
a token of remembrance at both weddings and funerals.
68–70. *bays . . . lightning*] A wreath of bays was given to a conqueror or
poet in token of success; the bay tree was thought to give protection from
lightning.
70. *sheet*] i.e. winding-sheet (kept perhaps for her own funeral).

Zanche. Her ladyship's foolish.

Lady.   Alas! Her grief   75
    Hath turned her child again.

Cornelia.   You're very welcome.
    There's rosemary for you, and rue for you,

                                To FLAMINEO.

    Heart's-ease for you. I pray make much of it.
    I have left more for myself.

Francisco.   Lady, who's this?

Cornelia. You are, I take it, the grave-maker.

Flamineo.   So.   80

Zanche. 'Tis Flamineo.

Cornelia. Will you make me such a fool? Here's a white hand.
      CORNELIA *doth this in several forms of distraction.*
    Can blood so soon be washed out? Let me see:
    When screech-owls croak upon the chimney-tops,
    And the strange cricket i'th'oven sings and hops,   85
    When yellow spots do on your hands appear,
    Be certain then you of a corse shall hear.
    Out upon't, how 'tis speckled! H'as handled a toad,
    sure.
    Cowslip-water is good for the memory; pray buy me   90
    three ounces of't.

Flamineo. I would I were from hence.

Cornelia.   Do you hear, sir?
    I'll give you a saying which my grandmother
    Was wont, when she heard the bell toll, to sing o'er
    Unto her lute.

Flamineo.   Do an you will, do.   95

Cornelia. Call for the robin-red-breast and the wren,
    Since o'er shady groves they hover,

---

    77. *rue*] The shrub had bitter leaves and was often associated with *rue* =
'sorrow, regret'.

    77.1. *To* FLAMINEO] so placed in the Quarto; she probably gives the rue to
him, the other herbs to bystanders.

    78. *Heart's-ease*] pansies.

    88. *toad*] thought to have poisonous venom, which was dangerous in
proportion to the number of spots to be seen under its womb.

    95. *an*] if.

    96. *robin-red-breast*] Finding a dead body, the bird was said to cover the
face, or even the whole body, with moss.

    wren] believed to be the robin's wife.

And with leaves and flow'rs do cover
The friendless bodies of unburied men.
Call unto his funeral dole   100
The ant, the field-mouse, and the mole
To rear him hillocks, that shall keep him warm,
And (when gay tombs are robbed) sustain no harm;
But keep the wolf far thence, that's foe to men,
For with his nails he'll dig them up agen.   105
They would not bury him 'cause he died in a quarrel,
But I have an answer for them.
Let holy church receive him duly,
Since he paid the church tithes truly.
His wealth is summed, and this is all his store: 110
This poor men get; and great men get no more.
Now the wares are gone, we may shut up shop.
Bless you all, good people,—

          Exeunt CORNELIA[, ZANCHE,] *and* Ladies.

Flamineo. I have a strange thing in me, to th'which
I cannot give a name, without it be   115
Compassion. I pray, leave me.

          Exit FRANCISCO.

This night I'll know the utmost of my fate;
I'll be resolved what my rich sister means
T'assign me for my service. I have lived
Riotously ill, like some that live in court;   120
And sometimes, when my face was full of smiles,
Have felt the maze of conscience in my breast.
Oft gay and honoured robes those tortures try;

---

100. *dole*] funeral rites.
104–5.] supposed sign of death by murder; see *The Duchess of Malfi*,
IV.ii.309–11: 'The wolf shall find her grave, and scrape it up: / Not to devour
the corpse, but to discover / The horrid murder.'
105. *agen*] again; the original spelling is retained for the rhyme.
110. *summed*] reckoned, brought into small compass.
111.] i.e. The poor and the wealthy are equal in death.
112. *we . . . shop*] The stage-curtains were probably closed at this point;
see l. 65.S.D. and n. above.
115. *without it be*] unless it is.
118. *resolved*] assured, satisfied.
122. *maze*] bewilderment or, perhaps, windings.
123.] While the general sense is clear (that even great men must endure

We think cagèd birds sing, when indeed they cry.

Enter BRACCIANO's Ghost, *in his leather cassock and breeches,
    boots, [and] a cowl, [in his hand] a pot of lily-flowers
                with a skull in 't.*

Ha! I can stand thee. Nearer, nearer yet.   125
What a mockery hath death made of thee?
Thou look'st sad.
In what place art thou? In yon starry gallery,
Or in the cursèd dungeon? No? Not speak?
Pray, sir, resolve me, what religion's best   130
For a man to die in? Or is it in your knowledge
To answer me how long I have to live?
That's the most necessary question.
Not answer? Are you still like some great men
That only walk like shadows up and down,   135
And to no purpose? Say:— *The Ghost throws earth upon
                              him and shows him the skull.*
What's that? O fatal! He throws earth upon me,
A dead man's skull beneath the roots of flowers.
I pray speak, sir,—our Italian churchmen
Make us believe dead men hold conference   140
With their familiars, and many times
Will come to bed to them, and eat with them.
                                        Exit Ghost.
He's gone; and see, the skull and earth are vanished.
This is beyond melancholy.

---

torments of conscience), the precise meaning is obscure: either *robes* = 'great
men' and *try* = 'experience, undergo', or *tortures* is the subject of the sentence
and *try* = 'test the effect of'.

  124.1. leather cassock] long coat or cloak especially as worn by soldiers;
customary dress for a stage ghost.

  124.2. cowl] To be buried in a friar's cowl was supposed to bring remission of sins.

  pot of lily-flowers] a common emblem: in G. Wither, *Emblems* (1635), Vice
is depicted with a pot of lily flowers and a skull with cross-bones by her side,
promising Youth 'what the wanton flesh desires to have'; a pot with a
flowering lily is found in many depictions of the Annunciation.

  125. *stand*] withstand.

  141. *familiars*] i.e. friends still on earth.

  144. *beyond melancholy*] i.e. more than a figment of my own imagination;

I do dare my fate   145
To do its worst. Now to my sister's lodging,
And sum up all these horrors: the disgrace
The prince threw on me; next, the piteous sight
Of my dead brother; and my mother's dotage;
And last this terrible vision. All these   150
Shall with Vittoria's bounty turn to good,
Or I will drown this weapon in her blood.   *Exit.*

[v. v]

> *Enter* FRANCISCO, LODOVICO, *and* HORTENSIO
> [*overhearing them*].

Lodovico. My lord, upon my soul you shall no further;
You have most ridiculously engaged yourself
Too far already. For my part, I have paid
All my debts, so if I should chance to fall
My creditors fall not with me; and I vow   5
To quite all in this bold assembly
To the meanest follower. My lord, leave the city,
Or I'll forswear the murder.
Francisco.   Farewell, Lodovico.
If thou dost perish in this glorious act,
I'll rear unto thy memory that fame   10
Shall in the ashes keep alive thy name.
> [*Exeunt* FRANCISCO *and* LODOVICO *severally.*]
Hortensio. There's some black deed on foot. I'll presently
Down to the citadel, and raise some force.
These strong court factions that do brook no checks,
In the career oft break the riders' necks.   [*Exit.*] 15

---

despair was considered the next stage of derangement beyond 'melancholy'.

V.v.6. *quite*] repay, requite.
7. *To*] down to, including.
meanest] of lowest social station.
8. *forswear*] forswear my promise to commit.
10. *rear*] foster, raise like a monument.
11. *Shall*] i.e. which shall.
12. *presently*] at once, immediately.
14. *brook no checks*] tolerate no opposition.
15. *career*] short gallop at full speed.

[v. vi]

Enter VITTORIA *with a book in her hand;* ZANCHE,
[*and*] FLAMINEO, *following them.*

Flamineo. What, are you at your prayers? Give o'er.
Vittoria.   How, ruffin?
Flamineo. I come to you 'bout worldly business.
  Sit down, sit down. Nay, stay, blowze, you may hear it;
  The doors are fast enough.
Vittoria.   Ha, are you drunk?
Flamineo. Yes, yes, with wormwood water. You shall taste   5
  Some of it presently.
Vittoria.   What intends the fury?
Flamineo. You are my lord's executrix, and I claim
  Reward for my long service.
Vittoria.   For your service?
Flamineo. Come, therefore, here is pen and ink; set down
  What you will give me.   *She writes.*   10
Vittoria. There,—
Flamineo.   Ha! Have you done already?—
  'Tis a most short conveyance.
Vittoria.   I will read it.
  [*Reads*] '*I give that portion to thee, and no other,*
  Which Cain groaned under, having slain his brother.'
Flamineo. A most courtly patent to beg by.   15
Vittoria. You are a villain.
Flamineo. Is't come to this? They say affrights cure agues.

V.vi.0.1. book] Flamineo's first words suggest that this is a devotional
book; but not necessarily so, because an entry with a book, on the stage at
this time, was used very commonly as a sign of melancholy (*Hamlet* provides
a well-known example).

  1. *ruffin*] devil (cant term), ruffian.
  3. *blowze*] fat, red-faced girl; here used, ironically, of the black-faced
Zanche.
  5. *wormwood*] a bitter-tasting herb; emblem of what is mortifying to the
soul.
  6. *intends*] signifies.
  12. *conveyance*] document transfering property.
  14. Cain] cursed by God for killing his brother; see Genesis iv.11–12.
  15. *patent*] see V.i.112n.
  17. *agues*] fevers.

Thou hast a devil in thee; I will try
If I can scare him from thee.—Nay, sit still;
My lord hath left me yet two case of jewels   20
Shall make me scorn your bounty; you shall see them.
                                                    [*Exit.*]

Vittoria. Sure he's distracted.
Zanche.   O, he's desperate;
For your own safety give him gentle language.

        [*Re-*]*enter* [FLAMINEO] *with two case of pistols.*

Flamineo. Look, these are better far at a dead lift
Than all your jewel house.
Vittoria.   And yet methinks   25
These stones have no fair lustre; they are ill set.
Flamineo. I'll turn the right side towards you; you shall see
How they will sparkle.
Vittoria.   Turn this horror from me.
What do you want? What would you have me do?
Is not all mine, yours? Have I any children?   30
Flamineo. Pray thee, good woman, do not trouble me
With this vain worldly business; say your prayers.
I made a vow to my deceasèd lord
Neither yourself nor I should outlive him
The numb'ring of four hours.
Vittoria.   Did he enjoin it?   35
Flamineo. He did, and 'twas a deadly jealousy,
Lest any should enjoy thee after him,
That urged him vow me to it. For my death,
I did propound it voluntarily, knowing
If he could not be safe in his own court   40
Being a great duke, what hope then for us?
Vittoria. This is your melancholy and despair.
Flamineo.   Away!
Fool thou art to think that politicians

---

20. *case*] pair.
24. *dead lift*] lifting of a 'dead' weight (a common phrase for 'sudden
emergency'); with an obvious pun on *dead*.
26. *stones*] (1) precious stones, jewels; (2) gun-stones (used for shot).
28. *sparkle*] i.e. in an explosion of gunpowder.

Do use to kill the effects of injuries
And let the cause live. Shall we groan in irons,   45
Or be a shameful and a weighty burden
To a public scaffold? This is my resolve:
I would not live at any man's entreaty
Nor die at any's bidding.
Vittoria.   Will you hear me?
Flamineo. My life hath done service to other men,   50
    My death shall serve mine own turn; make you ready—
Vittoria. Do you mean to die indeed?
Flamineo.   With as much pleasure
    As e'er my father gat me.
Vittoria. [*Aside*] Are the doors locked?
Zanche. [*Aside*] Yes, madam.   55
Vittoria. Are you grown an atheist? Will you turn your body,
    Which is the goodly palace of the soul,
    To the soul's slaughter house? O, the cursèd devil
    Which doth present us with all other sins
    Thrice candied o'er, despair with gall and stibium,   60
    Yet we carouse it off—[*Aside to Zanche*] cry out for help—
    Makes us forsake that which was made for man,
    The world, to sink to that was made for devils,
    Eternal darkness.
Zanche.   Help, help!
Flamineo.   I'll stop your throat
    With winter plums,—
Vittoria.   I prithee yet remember   65
    Millions are now in graves which at last day

---

44. *use*] make it their practice.

57. *goodly . . . soul*] In a devotional context, the body was usually spoken of as the soul's prison.

58–61. *the cursèd . . . off*] i.e. The devil makes all sins, except despair, seem sweet and attractive to the taste, but offers despair mixed with bitterness and poison; nevertheless we commit suicide willingly. *Stibium* is a poisonous metallic antimony; see II.i.285.

64. *stop your throat*] gag you.

65. *winter plums*] an obscure phrase; because plums are a summer fruit and none will keep until winter unless dried or otherwise preserved. However the general sense of the passage seems clear: Zanche will be choked with some hard and bitter fruit.

Like mandrakes shall rise shrieking.

Flamineo.   Leave your prating,
For these are but grammatical laments,
Feminine arguments, and they move me
As some in pulpits move their auditory   70
More with their exclamation than sense
Of reason, or sound doctrine.

Zanche. [*Aside*]   Gentle madam,
Seem to consent, only persuade him teach
The way to death; let him die first.

Vittoria. [*Aside*] 'Tis good, I apprehend it.—   75
[*Aloud*] To kill one's self is meat that we must take
Like pills, not chew't, but quickly swallow it;
The smart a'th'wound, or weakness of the hand
May else bring treble torments.

Flamineo.   I have held it
A wretched and most miserable life,   80
Which is not able to die.

Vittoria.   O, but frailty!
Yet I am now resolved. Farewell, affliction!
Behold, Bracciano, I that while you lived
Did make a flaming altar of my heart
To sacrifice unto you, now am ready   85
To sacrifice heart and all. Farewell, Zanche.

Zanche. How, madam? Do you think that I'll outlive you?
Especially when my best self Flamineo
Goes the same voyage?

Flamineo.   O most lovèd Moor!

Zanche. Only by all my love let me entreat you—   90
Since it is most necessary none of us
Do violence on ourselves—let you or I
Be her sad taster, teach her how to die.

Flamineo. Thou dost instruct me nobly. Take these pistols;

---

67. *mandrakes*] said to shriek when pulled from the ground; here the image is apocalyptic.

68. *grammatical*] (1) merely of words and sound; (2) according to rule and, therefore, elementary.

71. *exclamation*] (1) formal declamation; (2) vociferation.

93. *taster*] Kings ate only after their food had been tested for possible poison.

Because my hand is stained with blood already,   95
Two of these you shall level at my breast,
Th'other 'gainst your own, and so we'll die,
Most equally contented; but first swear
Not to outlive me.
Vittoria and Zanche.   Most religiously.
Flamineo. Then here's an end of me. Farewell, daylight,   100
And O contemptible physic! that dost take
So long a study only to preserve
So short a life, I take my leave of thee.
These are two cupping-glasses, that shall draw
                              Showing the pistols.
All my infected blood out. Are you ready?   105
Vittoria and Zanche. Ready.
Flamineo. Whither shall I go now? O Lucian, thy ridiculous
purgatory! To find Alexander the Great cobbling shoes,
Pompey tagging points, and Julius Caesar making hair
buttons; Hannibal selling blacking, and Augustus crying   110
garlic, Charlemagne selling lists by the dozen, and King
Pippin crying apples in a cart drawn with one horse!
Whether I resolve to fire, earth, water, air,
Or all the elements by scruples, I know not
Nor greatly care,—Shoot, shoot,   115
Of all deaths the violent death is best,
For from ourselves it steals ourselves so fast

---

97. *Th'other . . . own*] i.e. the second pair of pistols will kill Zanche and
Vittoria.

104. *cupping-glasses*] surgical vessels in which a vacuum was created by the
application of heat, and thus used to draw off blood.

107–12. *Lucian . . . horse*] taken from Lucian's *Menippos*.

109. *tagging points*] Tagged laces (*points*) were a common means of fasten-
ing garments.

109–10. *hair buttons*] buttons made of hair.

110. *blacking*] lamp-black, used to give a shining black surface to boots
and shoes.

crying] calling out the price of.

111. *lists*] strips of cloth, used as garters, ties, etc.

112. *Pippin*] Pepin ('The Short'), King of the Franks (d. 768); with a pun
on the 'pippin' apple.

113. *resolve*] dissolve.

114. *scruples*] small portions.

The pain once apprehended is quite past.

They shoot and run to him and tread upon him.

Vittoria. What—are you dropt?

Flamineo. I am mixed with earth already; as you are noble,   120
Perform your vows, and bravely follow me.

Vittoria. Whither—to hell?

Zanche.   To most assured damnation.

Vittoria. O thou most cursèd devil!

Zanche.   Thou art caught—

Vittoria. In thine own engine; I tread the fire out
That would have been my ruin.   125

Flamineo. Will you be perjured? What a religious oath was
Styx that the gods never durst swear by and violate? O,
that we had such an oath to minister, and to be so well
kept in our courts of justice!

Vittoria. Think whither thou art going.

Zanche.   And remember   130
What villainies thou hast acted.

Vittoria.   This thy death
Shall make me like a blazing ominous star,—
Look up and tremble.

Flamineo.   O, I am caught with a springe!

Vittoria. You see the fox comes many times short home;
'Tis here proved true.

Flamineo.   Killed with a couple of braches.   135

Vittoria. No fitter off'ring for the infernal Furies
Than one in whom they reigned while he was living.

Flamineo. O the way's dark and horrid! I cannot see,—
Shall I have no company?

Vittoria.   O, yes, thy sins

---

124. *engine*] contrivance, plot.

127. *Styx*] When a god was to be bound by an oath, Iris would collect
water from this river in Hades and take it back to Olympia as witness.

131-2. *This . . . star*] Comets were regarded as omens of disaster.

133. *springe*] snare (for catching small game).

134. *the fox . . . home*] i.e. even the cunning fox may fail to return with its
prey.

135. *with*] by.
braches] bitches.

136-7.] There could be no fitter offering to the infernal spirits of revenge
than one like Flamineo who was possessed by them in his life.

Do run before thee to fetch fire from hell,   140
  To light thee thither.
Flamineo.   O, I smell soot,
  Most stinking soot, the chimney is a-fire,—
  My liver's parboiled like Scotch holy bread;
  There's a plumber laying pipes in my guts,—it scalds;
  Wilt thou outlive me?
Zanche.   Yes, and drive a stake   145
  Through thy body; for we'll give it out
  Thou didst this violence upon thyself.
Flamineo. O cunning devils! Now I have tried your love,
  And doubled all your reaches. I am not wounded;

                              FLAMINEO *riseth.*

  The pistols held no bullets; 'twas a plot   150
  To prove your kindness to me; and I live
  To punish your ingratitude. I knew
  One time or other you would find a way
  To give me a strong potion.—O men
  That lie upon your death-beds, and are haunted   155
  With howling wives, ne'er trust them; they'll re-marry
  Ere the worm pierce your winding-sheet; ere the spider
  Make a thin curtain for your epitaphs.
  How cunning you were to discharge! Do you practise
  at the Artillery Yard? Trust a woman?—Never, never.   160
  Bracciano be my precedent; we lay our souls to pawn to
  the devil for a little pleasure, and a woman makes the
  bill of sale. That ever man should marry! For one

---

143. *parboiled*] partially boiled.
Scotch holy bread] stewed sheep's liver.
145–6. *drive . . . body*] Suicides were traditionally buried at crossroads
with a stake driven through the heart to restrain their evil ghosts.
149. *doubled . . . reaches*] equalled and so outstripped all your efforts, plots.
151. *prove*] test.
kindness] natural affection.
160. *Artillery Yard*] Under the leadership of Philip Hudson, a Lieutenant
in the Artillery Company, the 'weekly exercise of arms and military disci-
pline' for citizens and merchants was revived in 1610 at the Artillery Gardens,
Bishopgate; official recognition from the Privy Council followed on 3 July
1612. Flamineo alludes to the zeal and inexperience of the unprofessional
soldiers; cf. the first scene (often attributed to Webster) of *Anything for a
Quiet Life* (c. 1620–21): 'At the Artillery Garden, one of my neighbours, in
courtesy to salute me with his musket, set afire my breeches'.

Hypermnestra that saved her lord and husband, forty-
nine of her sisters cut their husbands' throats all in one   165
night. There was a shoal of virtuous horse-leeches.
Here are two other instruments.

Vittoria.   Help, help!

Enter LODOVICO, GASPARO, [*disguised as Capuchins,*] PEDRO,
[*and*] CARLO.

Flamineo. What noise is that? Hah? False keys i'th'court!
Lodovico. We have brought you a masque.
Flamineo.   A matachin, it seems,
By your drawn swords. Churchmen turned revellers!   170
Carlo. Isabella, Isabella!
Lodovico. Do you know us now?
                    [*They throw off their disguises.*]
Flamineo.   Lodovico and Gasparo.
Lodovico. Yes, and that Moor the duke gave pension to
Was the great Duke of Florence.
Vittoria.   O, we are lost.
Flamineo. You shall not take justice from forth my hands;   175
O, let me kill her!—I'll cut my safety
Through your coats of steel. Fate's a spaniel;

---

164. *Hypermnestra*] The fifty daughters of Danaus were commanded to
marry the fifty sons of their father's brother, Aegyptus; when Danaus was
warned by an oracle that he would be killed by one of his nephews, he
persuaded his daughters to murder their husbands on the marriage night. All
obeyed except Hypermnestra, who spared her husband Lynceus.

166. *virtuous*] said sarcastically.

horse-leeches] blood-suckers.

167. *two other instruments*] i.e. two more pistols; presumably Flamineo is
overpowered before he is able to use them. To manage this and the later
business in the scene, and to make up numbers for a 'masque' (l. 169), at
least four conspirators should enter; Flamineo is not aware of them until after
'What noise is that?' (l. 168). Contemporary accounts of Vittoria's death note
that a 'band' of masked men entered.

168. *keys*] Presumably Flamineo had locked a door behind him to prevent
his victims' escape.

169. *masque*] formal and, often, surprise entry of disguised and masked
revellers, who then invited those already present to dance with them.

matachin] sword-dance, in masks and fantastic costumes.

171. *Isabella!*] i.e. We come in the name of Isabella, to avenge her death.

177–8. *Fate's . . . from us*] i.e. Fate dogs us at our heels, and our earnest
efforts cannot rid us of it.

We cannot beat it from us. What remains now?
Let all that do ill take this precedent:
Man may his fate foresee, but not prevent.   180
And of all axioms this shall win the prize:
'Tis better to be fortunate than wise.

Gasparo. Bind him to the pillar.

Vittoria.   O, your gentle pity!—
I have seen a blackbird that would sooner fly
To a man's bosom than to stay the gripe   185
Of the fierce sparrow-hawk.

Gasparo.   Your hope deceives you.

Vittoria. If Florence be i'th'court, would he would kill me!

Gasparo. Fool! Princes give rewards with their own hands,
But death or punishment by the hands of others.

Lodovico. Sirrah, you once did strike me; I'll strike you   190
Into the centre.

Flamineo. Thou'lt do it like a hangman, a base hangman,
Not like a noble fellow, for thou seest
I cannot strike again.

Lodovico.   Dost laugh?

Flamineo. Wouldst have me die, as I was born, in whining?   195

Gasparo. Recommend yourself to heaven.

Flamineo. No, I will carry mine own commendations thither.

Lodovico. O, could I kill you forty times a day
And use't four year together, 'twere too little;
Nought grieves but that you are too few to feed   200
The famine of our vengeance. What dost think on?

Flamineo. Nothing; of nothing. Leave thy idle questions.

---

183. *pillar*] possibly part of the structure of the tiring-house façade; but for *The Virgin Martyr* (1620) a special pillar was erected on the stage of the Red Bull.

184–6. *I . . . sparrow-hawk*] Vittoria tries to flatter the assassins by suggesting that they are more humane than her own brother.

185. *stay*] await.

187. *Florence*] the Duke of Florence.

188–9.] Gasparo scornfully points out that if the Duke of Florence wanted Vittoria dead, he would hire agents rather than kill her himself.

191. *the centre*] i.e. the heart.

194. *I . . . again*] Flamineo's arms were bound after l. 183.

196–7.] Gasparo says, in effect, 'Say your prayers in preparation for death.' Flamineo answers, 'No, I'll do that myself when I get there.'

I am i'th'way to study a long silence;
To prate were idle. I remember nothing.
There's nothing of so infinite vexation   205
As man's own thoughts.

Lodovico.   O thou glorious strumpet,
Could I divide thy breath from this pure air
When't leaves thy body, I would suck it up
And breathe't upon some dunghill.

Vittoria.   You, my death's-man!
Methinks thou dost not look horrid enough;   210
Thou hast too good a face to be a hangman.
If thou be, do thy office in right form;
Fall down upon thy knees and ask forgiveness.

Lodovico. O, thou hast been a most prodigious comet,
But I'll cut off your train.—Kill the Moor first.   215

Vittoria. You shall not kill her first. Behold my breast,—
I will be waited on in death; my servant
Shall never go before me.

Gasparo. Are you so brave?

Vittoria.   Yes I shall welcome death
As princes do some great ambassadors;   220
I'll meet thy weapon half way.

Lodovico.   Thou dost tremble;
Methinks fear should dissolve thee into air.

Vittoria. O thou art deceived, I am too true a woman;
Conceit can never kill me. I'll tell thee what:
I will not in my death shed one base tear,   225
Or if look pale, for want of blood, not fear.

Carlo. Thou art my task, black Fury.

Zanche.   I have blood
As red as either of theirs; wilt drink some?
'Tis good for the falling sickness. I am proud
Death cannot alter my complexion,   230

---

204. *idle*] useless, foolish.

206. *glorious*] vainglorious.

213.] Executioners conventionally asked forgiveness of their victims.

215. *train*] (1) tail of a comet; (2) retinue (i.e. Zanche).

224. *Conceit*] (1) apprehension, fantasy; (2) vanity; (3) conception.

227–8. *blood . . . theirs*] Red blood was a sign of courage. Zanche proudly insists that, though black, she is as brave as the other victims.

229. *falling sickness*] epilepsy, with wordplay on 'falling' down dead.

For I shall ne'er look pale.

Lodovico.   Strike, strike,
 With a joint motion.   [*They strike.*]
Vittoria.   'Twas a manly blow.
 The next thou giv'st, murder some sucking infant,
 And then thou wilt be famous.
Flamineo.   O, what blade is't?
 A Toledo, or an English fox?   235
 I ever thought a cutler should distinguish
 The cause of my death, rather than a doctor.
 Search my wound deeper; tent it with the steel
 That made it.
Vittoria. O my greatest sin lay in my blood.   240
 Now my blood pays for't.
Flamineo.   Th'art a noble sister—
 I love thee now; if woman do breed man
 She ought to teach him manhood. Fare thee well.
 Know many glorious women that are famed
 For masculine virtue have been vicious,   245
 Only a happier silence did betide them;
 She hath no faults, who hath the art to hide them.
Vittoria. My soul, like to a ship in a black storm,
 Is driven I know not whither.
Flamineo.   Then cast anchor.
 Prosperity doth bewitch men seeming clear,   250

---

231. *pale*] i.e. with fear. Being black, she cannot look pale.

232. *manly*] spoken with bitter irony.

235. *fox*] a kind of sword.

236. *cutler*] Flamineo taunts his assassins by giving credit for his death to the person who made the sword, not to the one who uses it.

238-9.] Both *Search* and *tent* = 'to probe, cleanse'; but the latter also carries wordplay on *tend* = 'care for'.

240-1. *blood . . . blood*] i.e. 'passion . . . life-blood'; see I.ii.292 and n. This 'passion' could be either sexual passion or, more generally, a temperamental vitality; the inherent ambiguity can be resolved only in performance, if then.

244-7. *Know . . . them*] Know that many wonderful women, who are renowned for courage, have, in fact, been vicious, only a more fortunate silence has looked after their reputation—that a woman who has the skill to hide her faults appears to have none.

250-1.] When all goes well we can see no danger under the calm sea, but the great waves of a storm laugh at us as they break on the rocks and show perils near at hand.

But seas do laugh, show white, when rocks are near.
We cease to grieve, cease to be Fortune's slaves,
Nay, cease to die by dying. Art thou gone,
And thou so near the bottom?—False report
Which says that women vie with the nine Muses   255
For nine tough durable lives. I do not look
Who went before, nor who shall follow me;
No, at myself I will begin and end:
While we look up to heaven we confound
Knowledge with knowledge. O, I am in a mist.   260
Vittoria. O happy they that never saw the court,
    Nor ever knew great man but by report. VITTORIA *dies.*
Flamineo. I recover like a spent taper for a flash
    And instantly go out.

Let all that belong to great men remember th'old wives'   265
tradition, to be like the lions i'th'Tower on Candlemas
day, to mourn if the sun shine, for fear of the pitiful
remainder of winter to come.

'Tis well yet there's some goodness in my death,
My life was a black charnel. I have caught   270
An everlasting cold. I have lost my voice
Most irrecoverably. Farewell, glorious villains;
This busy trade of life appears most vain,

---

253. *cease . . . dying*] i.e. once dead we suffer no more pain. Compare
Julius Caesar, II.ii.32–3: 'Cowards die many times before their deaths; / The
valiant never taste of death but once.'

253–4. *thou . . . thou*] i.e. Zanche . . . Vittoria.

259–60. *While . . . knowledge.*] When we turn our thoughts to heaven, we
confuse (or undermine, destroy) one set of thoughts with another.

260. *mist*] Cf. *The Duchess of Malfi*, V.v.93–6: 'How came Antonio by his
death? / *Bosola.* In a mist: I know not how— / Such a mistake as I have often
seen / In a play . . .' See also Marlowe, *II Tamburlaine*, II.iv, where Zenocrate
is said to be 'All dazzled with the hellish mists of death'.

265–8.] There was a small zoo in the Tower of London. *Candlemas* is 2
February; cf. the proverb, 'If Candlemas day be fair and bright, winter will
have another flight', i.e. last some six weeks longer. Flamineo warns his
audience that all men of noble spirit (lions are the king of beasts) will enjoy
only brief happiness if they live at the service of powerful men at court.

270. *charnel*] charnel house, where the bones of the dead were stored.

272. *glorious*] (1) boastful; (2) famous (because they are his assassins).

273. *trade*] habitual practice, employment (often without any idea of
commerce).

most vain] (1) quite useless, empty; (2) full of vanity, conceited.

Since rest breeds rest, where all seek pain by pain.
Let no harsh flattering bells resound my knell,   275
Strike thunder, and strike loud to my farewell.   *Dies.*
English Ambassador. [*Within*] This way, this way, break ope
    the doors, this way.
Lodovico. Ha, are we betrayed?—
    Why then let's constantly die all together,
    And having finished this most noble deed,   280
    Defy the worst of fate, not fear to bleed.

    Enter Ambassadors and GIOVANNI [*with* Guards].

English Ambassador. Keep back the prince.—Shoot, shoot!
           [*They shoot, and wound* LODOVICO.]
Lodovico.   O, I am wounded.
    I fear I shall be ta'en.
Giovanni.   You bloody villains,
    By what authority have you committed
    This massacre?
Lodovico.   By thine.
Giovanni.   Mine?
Lodovico.   Yes, thy uncle,   285
    Which is a part of thee, enjoined us to't.
    Thou know'st me, I am sure,—I am Count Lodowick,
    And thy most noble uncle in disguise
    Was last night in thy court.
Giovanni.   Ha!
Carlo.   Yes, that Moor
    Thy father chose his pensioner.
Giovanni.   He turned murderer?   290
    Away with them to prison, and to torture;
    All that have hands in this shall taste our justice,
    As I hope heaven.
Lodovico.   I do glory yet

    274.] This might mean, simplistically, 'taking things easily brings content-
ment, whereas taking trouble only leads to trouble'; but this gloss scarcely
does justice to *breeds* and *seek*. Flamineo probably means that taking one's
ease only leads to more ease (i.e. to death), in a world where everyone who
makes great effort is, in effect, seeking their own misery and suffering (or the
need for yet more effort).
    276.] Cf. I.i.11–12.
    279. *constantly*] resolutely.
    293. *hope heaven*] hope to be saved.

That I can call this act mine own. For my part,
The rack, the gallows, and the torturing wheel　　　　295
Shall be but sound sleeps to me. Here's my rest;
I limbed this night-piece and it was my best.
Giovanni. Remove the bodies. See, my honoured lord,
What use you ought make of their punishment.
Let guilty men remember their black deeds　　　　300
Do lean on crutches, made of slender reeds.　*[Exeunt.]*

Instead of an epilogue only this of Martial supplies me:
Haec fuerint nobis praemia si placui.

For the action of the play, 'twas generally well, and I dare affirm,
with the joint testimony of some of their own quality, (for the true
imitation of life, without striving to make nature a monster) the best
that ever became them; whereof as I make a general acknowledgement, so in particular I must remember the well approved industry
of my friend Master Perkins, and confess the worth of his action did
crown both the beginning and end.

FINIS.

---

296. *rest*] (1) sleep; (2) final hope, resolution.
297. *limbed*] a seventeenth-century form of 'limned' (i.e. 'painted, por-
trayed'); this spelling quibblingly associates the word with the human bodies
which lie dead.
night-piece] painting depicting a night-scene.
299. *ought*] ought to.
301.2.] These things will be our reward, if I have pleased you (Martial).
301.8. *Perkins*] See Introduction.